21 Crowds greet a train carrying released republican prisoners on Dublin's Westland Row, 1917.

20 The camp became fertile ground for the spreading of the revolutionary gospel, and later became known as the 'University of Revolution'.

46 ...at 'no point did the cabinet seem to worry about the advisability of training a vast number of potential dissidents'.

62

FILM—'[N]o other medium can provide the man who has something to say with so receptive and so enormous an audience,' ...

www.historyireland.com

ALL CHANGED, CHANGED UTTERLY?

BY **GEORGINA LARAGY**

The legacy of the Easter Rising was almost immediately obvious to those who had participated and to those who had watched from the sidelines. This is evident in the use of flag days as a fund-raising event by the Irish National Aid and Volunteers' Dependants' Fund (INAVDF) (Gillis, pp 16–19), in the early attempts to create a 'Patriot/ Republican Plot' in Glasnevin Cemetery (Dodd, pp 31–2) and in the mourning rosettes worn by Tipperary hurlers in June 1916 (McElligott, pp 53–6). These early commemorative movements foreshadow our current 'Decade of Centenaries'. But there are deeper legacy issues to be considered.

While contemporaries could not know how things would develop, it was clear that the Rising was not considered an isolated event, as Gillis notes here. Much had been made of previous rebellions in 1798, 1803, 1848 and 1867, but for the post-1916 rebels there was a clear sense that 1916 was an opportunity to be built upon, yet there was no clear sign pointing out where to move next. While some, including John Devoy, considered a second attempt at a German-supported rebellion as a way forward (aan de Weil, pp 49–51), others took their inspiration from the Bolshevik Revolution of 1917 (O'Connor, pp 42–5).

In the context of continued Continental war, and the ill-conceived repression of separatists by the British authorities, there was an influx of new members into organisations such as Sinn Féin, Cumann na mBan and the GAA. Political activism and associational culture became key features of this increased engagement with the Irish separatist movement. An important characteristic of Irish politics can be identified during this period—the political mobilisation of 1916–18 demonstrates the role that community, identity and fellowship continued to play in Irish society.

The emergence of new organisations and the invigoration of already operational bodies provide tangible evidence of the Rising's impact on political activism at a local and national level. This is testimony to the change in public opinion as well. The INAVDF emerged out of the Prisoners' Dependants' Fund and built on relationships with the already prominent, growing and increasingly active Cumann na mBan, Irish Volunteers and Na Fianna Éireann. The role of Cumann na mBan in the 1917 by-elections demonstrated the impact that women had on political life during this period, especially following their inclusion in the franchise in 1918.

Political ideologies that gained practical expression during this period included trade unionism, feminism, nationalism and republicanism, as McAuliffe (pp 46–8) and Yeates (pp 34–7) examine in their articles. This diversity in Irish political life punctured the stale crust that the Home Rule vs Unionism dichotomy had become. Many areas had not seen a proper election since the 1890s, with Irish Parliamentary Party (IPP) candidates standing unopposed in many constituencies. The emergence of a genuine nationalist alternative in Sinn Féin may have been unexpected, but these years were a short, sharp apprenticeship in the realities of political activism and success, which was what they needed after the surprise injection of support handed to them by the British authorities who mistakenly identified the Rising as a 'Sinn Féin rebellion'.

But Sinn Féin's electoral victory in December 1918 cannot be explained only by reference to their actions after the Rising. Roy Foster's *Vivid faces* (2014) points to a generational dimension, as youth began to push experience off the political platform. Marie Coleman demonstrates the very practical implications of the deaths of senior IPP MPs for the electoral map of Ireland, necessitating four by-elections in 1917 alone (pp 22–5). The reality that the IPP had become a stale political force is demonstrated by their adherence to Home Rule in the face of a changed political landscape, their conservatism and deference to Westminster, and their early support during the war for enlistment. Their involvement in the Irish Anti-Conscription Committee could not stop the sea change taking place in Irish politics.

The conscription crisis of 1918 made manifest the achievements of cooperation and unity on the political stage, as labour, suffragettes, Sinn Féin and the IPP coalesced in opposition to the extension of conscription to Ireland, which was thought necessary because the British armed forces were stretched to breaking point on the Western Front. Rather than securing continued Irish participation in the war effort, it was one of several own goals scored by the British authorities in Ireland in the early twentieth century. Postponing Home Rule in 1914, executing the rebels and imprisoning thousands after Easter 1916, and threatening conscription in 1918 only served to radicalise Irish nationalism until separatism became its central objective.

The international context that served to influence British reaction to events in Ireland is often overlooked.

Although commemorative events since 2014 have firmly reinserted the First World War into the Irish historical narrative, the influence of the war as regards decisions made in and about Ireland is not always well understood. The Irish rebellion was just one of a number that occurred across the war-torn empires. Rebellions and revolutions in South Africa in 1914, in the Middle East in 1916 and in Russia in 1917 meant that the warring powers had to keep looking in two directions, both within and beyond their imperial borders. Michael Kennedy's article on the war off the Irish coast (pp 38–41) demonstrates clearly how much there is to learn about just how close the European conflict came to Irish shores.

But the political ideologies of Bolshevism, nationalism and feminism were not the only things that spread in this world increasingly connected by trade, migration and war. As Beiner, Marsh and Milne demonstrate (pp 57–61), the deadly influenza virus was as globally destructive as the First World War had been. In Ireland the 'Spanish 'flu' has only just emerged from the historiographical shadows. What efforts will be made to remember the twentieth century's first pandemic in May 1918–April 1919?

Also significant, as Condon notes (pp 62–7), was the emergence of film and cinema in Ireland. The importance for success of a known actor and international production companies prefigured the global reach and impact of film by the later twentieth century. This power was tapped into mid-war by the British government with *The Battle of the Somme* (1916), which played across Ireland. Another nationally potent screening was the footage of Thomas Ashe's funeral, shown within hours of the event in the Bohemian Cinema in Phibsborough (Gibney, pp 26–30). A hitherto-unremarked-upon fact is that the destruction of Sackville Street during the Rising left space for the construction of several cinemas, such as the Metropole and the Grand Central, on that main thoroughfare.

The Decade of Centenaries has

thrown up a number of new commemorative sites previously subsumed within a fairly narrow heritage trail that saw the Rising linked to the GPO, Kilmainham Gaol and Arbour Hill. A new Necrology Wall at Glasnevin Cemetery, commemorating republicans and Crown forces as well as the ordinary civilians who were victims of the 1916 Rising, has created controversy, but it does point to a newer, more inclusive vision of the past. The renovation of Richmond Barracks and its inclusion in the commemorative landscape highlights further the complex relationship between British imperial and Irish nationalist history on this island. Throughout the nineteenth century this barracks was a site from where Irishmen left as British soldiers to help expand and protect the empire. In 1916 it also became the site of the courts martial where sixteen Irish nationalists were sentenced to death. The commemoration of the by-elections of 1917 and the general election of 1918 expands the focus beyond Dublin once again, as places like East Clare, Longford and East Cavan emerge as important signposts on the road to Sinn Féin's

landslide victory in December 1918 (Hanley, pp 86–9).

After the Treaty of 1921, the political pluralism of 1916–18 had all but disappeared, as another dichotomous paradigm emerged to frame Irish politics. This slim volume complicates the narrative about the post-1916 period with which most of us are familiar, beginning with McGarry's piece on the aftermath of Easter Week (pp 9–13). To what extent were unionism, Redmondite nationalism and the labour and suffragette movements all sacrificed during those years for the goal of an independent Ireland? And to what extent did this cripple politics in subsequent decades? Was the period June 1916–December 1918 a hiatus of sorts between two periods of conflict? Or a period when another future was possible?

Georgina Laragy is Glasnevin Trust Assistant Professor in Public History and Cultural Heritage, Trinity College, Dublin.

●

Above: The devastation at Abbey Street corner immediately after the end of the Rising, showing the ruins of the Dublin Bread Company. (NLI)

AFTER THE RISING

'Describing how residents emerged "as if spellbound" to view "the wreck of their once fine city", the *Irish Times* conveyed the Rising's disorienting impact as Dubliners came to terms with the scale of death and destruction in the capital.'

Image: Clery's and O'Connell Street in ruins. (UCD Archives)

Did the rebellion really alter the course of history?

'IRELAND CANNOT BE THE SAME': THE IMPACT OF THE EASTER RISING

BY **FEARGHAL McGARRY**

Easter 1916 is the major turning point in modern Irish history. The executions of the rebel leaders, an appalling blunder by the British authorities, shifted nationalist opinion from hostility towards the rebels to sympathy for their plight and, ultimately, their political cause. The manner in which the Rising was suppressed destroyed not only the Irish Parliamentary Party but also its political project of Home Rule and the possibility of a peaceful evolution to Irish independence.

Or so (most of) the history books tell us. But how plausible are these claims? Each assumption can readily be contested. British decision-makers were more likely indifferent to—rather than ignorant of—the likely consequences of their actions in Ireland. Rather than transforming popular opinion, the Rising may well have crystallised growing disenchantment with John Redmond's Irish Parliamentary Party (IPP). Did the rebellion really alter the course of history? The emergence of new nation-states from the wreckage of empire elsewhere in Europe suggests that political conflict in Ireland was always likely. If the Rising had not occurred, could a post-war Tory-dominated government have implemented Home Rule in the face of determined unionist opposition? And, if so, would it have led to Irish independence?

We can never know the answer to such counterfactual questions, but we can reconstruct in precise detail the responses and assumptions of the main actors in the immediate aftermath of the Rising. Across the political spectrum, reactions to this unforeseen convulsion were characterised by ambiguity, confusion and divisions. Rather than heralding popular support for a republic, the Rising's immediate impact—as W.B. Yeats observed on 8 May—seemed remarkably uncertain: 'As yet one knows nothing of the future except that it must be very unlike the past'.

Describing how residents emerged 'as if spellbound' to view 'the wreck of their once fine city', the *Irish Times* conveyed the Rising's disorienting impact as Dubliners came to terms with the scale of death and destruction in the capital. There was considerable confusion about what had just happened. Who had organised the rebellion, and why? Was it a riot (as the British press had misleadingly reported) or an abortive revolution? Press reports emphasised Germany's involvement and exa-

ggerated the role of the Irish Citizen Army. The *Irish Catholic*, for example, denounced the rebellion as 'partly socialistic' and 'partly alien', while local bodies and prominent clergymen, including the primate, Cardinal Michael Logue, condemned it as a mad or criminal enterprise.

The response of the authorities also gave rise to uncertainty. 'Nobody believes there will be any mercy shown,' James Stephens recorded after the rebels in the General Post Office surrendered; 'it is freely reported that they are shot in the street, or are taken to the nearest barracks and shot there.' Confusion and anxiety extended to those who suppressed the insurrection. The rebels met with anger and hostility from Crown forces, many of whom were Irish, but also with curiosity, sympathy, respect and even admiration. John Regan, a Catholic Royal Irish Regiment officer, encountered a contingent of rebels singing *God Save Ireland*: 'I seemed to hear the words, "What matter if for Erin's cause we fall", sung in deadly earnest for the first time. I was greatly impressed in spite of my antipathy towards them owing to the loss of some of my men.' One rebel recalled how an officer who initially berated them as traitors broke down in tears: 'Why didn't you wait till the war was over, and we'd all be with you?' Such ambivalent responses indicate the complexity of Irish attitudes to the rebellion.

On Monday 1 May the disgraced chief secretary for Ireland,

Right: Postcard showing an image of Sackville Street after the bombardment. (UCD Archives)

KILMAINHAM MAY 1916

Above: Kilmainham Gaol, May 1916—contemporary painting, artist unknown. (National Museum of Ireland)

Augustine Birrell, resigned, leaving General Maxwell in control as 'military governor'. The executions commenced two days later, while mass arrests proceeded across the country. In Roscommon, a town of fewer than 1,900 people that had witnessed no disturbances, an occupying force of 700 soldiers arrested 27 people. Around 3,500 people were arrested, over 2,500 of whom were interned. Owing to poor intelligence, they included not only rebels but also many nationalists without separatist connections. Engendering widespread animosity but little terror, Maxwell's crude response was widely viewed as a miscalculation. The Post Office secretary, Sir Arthur Hamilton Norway, who had urged the suppression of the Volunteer movement before the Rising, complained that the scale of coercion made discrimi-

nation impossible. If the rank and file of the rebels 'had been dismissed contemptuously to their homes and the leaders treated as lunatics', the IPP MP Stephen Gwynn optimistically claimed, 'the whole thing would have been over'.

Maxwell, a competent officer who had dealt with anti-colonial violence in Egypt and South Africa, believed that his decision to inflict 'the most severe sentences' on the leaders was justified by the gravity of the rebellion, Germany's involvement, the scale of destruction of life and property, and the need to demonstrate that attacks on 'the safety of the realm will not be tolerated'. Nor was he naïve about its consequences. Fearing that 'Irish sentimentality will turn these graves into martyrs' shrines', he refused to release the corpses of the executed and, as early as 13 May, warned British Prime Minister Herbert Asquith that 'the younger generation is likely to be more revolutionary'. Observing, the following month, that

it is 'becoming increasingly difficult to differentiate between a Nationalist and a Sinn Féiner', he predicted that 'few, if any, of existing Nationalist MPs would be re-elected'.

Having failed to anticipate how the use of courts martial and the authorities' unnecessary if dramatic declaration of martial law would be perceived, Maxwell was taken aback by the scale and speed at which 'a revulsion of feeling had set in', a response he blamed on the misrepresentation of his actions by politicians, journalists, priests and 'extreme women'. Potentially as damaging to British credibility was the cabinet's decision to combine coercion with a renewed effort to implement Home Rule (which had previously been parked 'for the duration'). Calling for a 'new departure', Asquith tasked David Lloyd George with reaching an agreement between unionists and the IPP. Widely regarded as a concession to revolutionary violence, this initiative reflected official alarm at the response to the rebellion in the

US and throughout the Empire. This dual policy of coercion and conciliation, the standard British response to Irish violence, resulted not from any misunderstanding of its likely consequences in Ireland but from the need to prioritise the wider war effort. By July 1916 the sclerotic administration at Dublin Castle had returned to business as usual, complacently ignoring the RIC inspector general's demand that volunteer militias, a principal cause of the rebellion, be disarmed.

The rapidly shifting popular mood would leave the IPP, perceived as pro-British owing to its support for enlistment and the Liberal alliance, hopelessly stranded. Much outrage centred on British double standards, given the government's earlier leniency towards Carson's UVF. As the *Freeman's Journal* (later) noted: 'The fact that the insurgents were sent to death by a government largely composed of the men who had set in motion the process of demoralisation that had ended in bloodshed utterly revolted the conscience of the country'. Public sympathy for the rebels was reflected, and shaped, by their growing identification with Catholicism. The *Catholic Bulletin* emphasised the executed leaders' piety, portraying

> **Maxwell was taken aback by the scale and speed at which 'a revulsion of feeling had set in', a response he blamed on the misrepresentation of his actions by politicians, journalists, priests and 'extreme women'.**

● Above right: Orders of General John Maxwell regulating the manufacture and sale of arms in Ireland in December 1918 under DORA. (NLI)

● Right: General John Maxwell standing with soldiers in a barracks square in Ireland, *c.* 1916. (NLI)

ORDER

I, GENERAL THE RIGHT HONOURABLE SIR J. G. MAXWELL, K.C.B.; K.C.M.G.; C.V.O.; D.S.O., Commanding-in-Chief the Forces in Ireland, in exercise of the powers conferred upon me as Competent Military Authority by Regulation 30 of the Defence of the Realm (Consolidation) Regulations hereby prohibit the manufacture, sale, transfer or disposal of fire-arms, part of fire-arms, Military arms, parts of Military arms, ammunition (including sporting ammunition for use in shot guns) or explosive substances or any class thereof, within the Area of IRELAND, except subject to the following conditions, viz :—

(1) That my consent in writing or the consent in writing of an Officer authorised by me for the purpose has been obtained for the proposed manufacture, sale, transfer or disposal of the said articles or any of them, after a full and true disclosure of the particulars of the proposed manufacture, sale, transfer or disposal of the said articles or any of them outside the Dublin Metropolitan Police District to the District Inspector of the Royal Irish Constabulary for the District, and inside the Dublin Metropolitan Police District to a Superintendent of the Dublin Metropolitan Police.

The Inspector General of the Royal Irish Constabulary and the Chief Commissioner of the Dublin Metropolitan Police, and County and District Inspectors of the Royal Irish Constabulary, and Superintendents of the Dublin Metropolitan Police are Officers authorised by me for the said purpose, and

(2) That any person selling the said articles or any of them shall provide and keep a Register showing the full particulars, description, and amount of all such articles purchased or sold by the said person, or which he or she has in his or her possession for sale, giving the names and full addresses of the persons from whom the said articles were purchased or to whom the said articles were sold and the dates of each transaction, which entries must be made within twenty-four hours after the sale or purchase; and the said Register shall be open for inspection at all times by the District Inspector of the Royal Irish Constabulary in each District, or by some member of the Royal Irish Constabulary authorized by him, or, in the Dublin Metropolitan Police Area, by any Superintendent or Inspector of the Dublin Metropolitan Police, or any member of the said Force authorized by such Superintendent; and any person so selling or keeping for sale or having in possession for sale any such articles as aforesaid, shall at all times, when so required by the aforesaid Police Authorities, show to the said Authorities all stock on hand of any such articles; and in case the purchaser is not known to the Vendor, the Vendor shall require the purchaser to furnish satisfactory particulars of identification (which shall be entered in the Register of sales), and to sign his name and address in the Register of sales.

The ORDERS of the Competent Military Authority for IRELAND made under Regulation 30 of the Defence of the Realm Regulations and dated 8th December, 1915; 25th February, 1916; and the 30th March, 1916, are hereby CANCELLED.

GIVEN UNDER MY HAND THIS 28th day of SEPTEMBER, 1916.

J. G. MAXWELL, General Competent Military Authority.

Above: British soldiers in Henry Street after the Rising. (NLI)

Opposite page: Drawing a direct line between the 1798 Rebellion and the 1916 Rising, this image by Francis Rigney was published in New York in 1916. (NLI)

them as Catholic martyrs. While this enabled the *Bulletin* to evade censorship, it also cast an event tainted by associations with Fenian anti-clericalism and socialism in a more reassuring light.

The first public manifestations of support for the rebels were also expressed through religious observances, such as the Month's Mind Masses in June and the distribution of Mass cards and mourning badges. Thirteen-year-old Charlie Dalton, who would become the youngest of

Michael Collins's assassins, experienced 'holiness and exultation' on visiting the ruins of the GPO. He recalled the 'wonderful, proud feeling, walking in the procession' of a requiem Mass, and the 'sacred interest' with which he treasured photographs of the dead leaders. The Catholic Church's recalibrated response reinforced this new mood. On 17 May Bishop O'Dwyer denounced Maxwell (who had foolishly asked the bishop to discipline two pro-rebel priests in his diocese) as a military dictator: 'your regime has been one of the worst and blackest chapters in the history of the misgovernment of this country'. In July the archbishop of Dublin publicly rebuked the IPP for its alliance with the Liberal Party.

Just as during the preceding Home Rule crisis, the outmanoeuvred

IPP leadership played a difficult hand poorly, while wilier Liberal politicians responded to the crisis by ruthlessly prioritising personal and party advantage. At Westminster John Dillon's praise for the bravery of the rebels and passionate denunciation of British repression—'You are washing out our whole life work in a sea of blood'—echoed popular sentiment but also struck many as a belated and inconsistent repudiation of IPP policy. By agreeing publicly in June to the principle of temporary six-county partition but failing to secure Home Rule, Redmond secured the worst possible outcome to Lloyd George's initiative. Stephen Gwynn claimed that the British government's failure to honour its commitment to implement Home Rule in return for extracting this damaging concession 'finished the constitutional party and overthrew Redmond's power'.

Whether Home Rule could have been secured centred on unionist calculations after the Rising. Like those of other political factions, unionist responses were characterised by mistaken assumptions and internal divisions. On 1 May the *Irish Times* confidently predicted that the 'Dublin insurrection of 1916 will pass into history with the equally unsuccessful insurrections of the past'. While remarkably unprescient, this editorial testifies to the unpredictable nature of the Rising's immediate impact. The rebellion usefully demonstrated the inherently disloyal character of Irish nationalism notwithstanding Redmond's slippery rhetoric, but it also posed challenges for unionists, including the danger that all volunteer movements would now be disarmed.

Anticipating the findings of the Royal Commission, unionists blamed the rebellion on Birrell's failure to suppress the Irish Volunteers before the insurrection. Many observers, though, including not a few southern unionists, believed that Carson's Volunteers were also responsible for the rebellion. 'It is the government as a whole that are to blame', General Maxwell confided to his wife. 'Ever since they winked at Ulster breaking the law they have been in difficulties.' For his part, Carson's response to the Rising was measured: 'it will be a matter requiring the greatest wisdom … dealing with these men', he declared. 'Whatever is done, let it be done, not in a moment of temporary excitement, but with due deliberation in regard to the past and to the future.' Other unionists showed less foresight. Asquith's Home Rule initiative collapsed not only because each side had received different assurances on partition but also owing to the powerful opposition of English unionists within the cabinet, such as Walter Long and Lord Lansdowne. Similar intransigence would bedevil subsequent attempts to reach political accommodations with nationalism, rarely to the long-term advantage of unionism.

Irish republicans, many of whom were imprisoned, were largely bystanders to these seismic changes. For them, as for other observers, the implications of the Rising's impact on Ireland's rapidly changing political landscape were unclear. 'We are too near the event to judge in proper perspective', Liam de Roiste cautiously noted in his diary on 9 May. Like Yeats, though, he believed that after 'the orgy of blood … Ireland cannot be the same'. One consequence of the rebellion was to further radicalise the Volunteers, as weak or cautious leaders were pushed aside by younger men. The resolve of Tomás MacCurtain was strengthened by the humiliation of being subjected to an enquiry into Cork's failure to rise: 'If I live I will redeem 1916'.

But even the most enthusiastic converts to the rebel cause—like John Moynihan, who wrote from Tralee to his brother Michael, a British army soldier, shortly after the executions— did not envisage immediate gains:

'I do not know what view you take of the rebellion. Probably if you did not condemn it on other grounds you would do so on the ground of its hopelessness. And yet was the rebellion a blunder? No doubt, from a practical point of view, it was … It may cost us a decade of oppression. But Pearse and M[a]cDonagh, Plunkett and McDermott are not

really dead; the men who sought to destroy them only succeed in giving them a power over the hearts and minds of men greater than ever they had before.'

It would only gradually become clear that the most important consequence of the Rising was to make a republic the agreed objective of a diverse range of advanced nationalist and separatist organisations. It would take eighteen months for this coalition of forces to coalesce around a single political party, but considerably longer to determine the nature of that republic and how it might be achieved.

Fearghal McGarry is Professor of History at Queen's University, Belfast.

Further reading

J. Borgonovo, *The dynamics of war and revolution: Cork City, 1916–1918* (Cork, 2013).

F. McGarry, *The Rising. Ireland: Easter 1916* (Oxford, 2016).

C. Townshend, *Easter 1916: the Irish rebellion* (London, 2005).

What happened to the prisoners?

PAYING THE PRICE FOR REBELLION

BY **SEÁN ENRIGHT**

After the rebellion came the trials. The surrendering prisoners and those rounded up in the provinces were funnelled through Richmond Barracks. In the chaotic sift that followed, 160 prisoners were selected for trial. The rest spent barely a day or two in Richmond Barracks before being marched to the North Wall and embarked onto cattle-boats. Some 1,857 prisoners were deported and interned without trial.

From Dublin, the internees were sent by cattle-boat to prisons in Britain as far apart as Aylesbury and Glasgow. Some were released after a few weeks. One was Patrick O'Kelly from Clontarf, who had been at Jacob's factory during Easter Week. A few weeks later, an order came through for the release of a prisoner by the same name: a Redmondite interned in error. O'Kelly took his

chance and walked free. A few secured release by providing satisfactory references. Others were freed after questions were raised in the Commons. One of these was James Kelly, a justice of the peace and a former high sheriff, who had been swept up with all the rest. The arresting officer was Sir Francis Vane, who assured Kelly's wife that no harm would come to her husband: 'I give my solemn word'. Sir Francis was an honourable man, but once the prisoner was taken to Portobello Barracks there was little that could be done for him. It took the authorities over three weeks to let him go. A photo taken on Kelly's release shows a gaunt, wild figure with blackened eyes and crumpled clothing, with not a trace of the fastidiously dressed man who went into captivity.

The prisoners who were tried and convicted were a very mixed bunch. Of the 160 prisoners tried the oldest was 59, the youngest was sixteen and only one was a woman. Among the Dublin prisoners who were tried and convicted there were four college professors, two solicitors, a handful of university students, journalists, printers, office workers, railwaymen and trade unionists like William Partridge and Peadar Doyle (later lord mayor of Dublin). Richard Hayes was a doctor and George Irvine was a Church of Ireland Sunday School teacher. There were also men like Harry Boland, a tailor's cutter, as well as plasterers, tradesmen, artisans and shop assistants. The convicted prisoners from the provinces included 33 from Galway, eleven from Wexford, a handful from Cork and Kerry and a few from Limerick: mainly farmers, agricultural labourers, a blacksmith, a few stonemasons and national schoolteachers. One, John Grady from Athenry, gave his occupation as 'car owner'.

Of the 160 prisoners tried, 154 were convicted and of these fifteen were executed. The remaining 139 prisoners were moved from Kilmainham to Mountjoy, where they had a hot bath and a mattress for the first time in weeks. They were then taken in a convoy of Black Marias to the North Wall, where families, well-wishers and dockers had gathered at the quayside.

One of the prisoners was William O'Dea, a 27-year-old Dubliner. He had been due to marry on Easter Monday. Faced with the choice of marriage or rebellion, he had turned out on Easter Monday and ended up at the Mendicity. He was tried and convicted a few days later but his death sentence had been commuted to penal servitude. Leaning against the ship rail, O'Dea spotted his fiancée on the quays, waving. He reached into his pocket and pulled out a ring; he gave it to an officer on the gangway and pointed at the girl. The ring passed from one pair of hands to another until it reached the girl. The crowd was briefly silent. She took the ring and the crowd cheered. O'Dea disappeared into the hold of the ship.

De Valera and the largest group of prisoners went to Dartmoor prison, where 'God is Love' was chiselled over the gatehouse. Here the prisoners were deloused. Some of the GPO prisoners had burn injuries and

found their bandages prised off with little care. Food was in short supply and discipline was unremittingly harsh: de Valera was put in isolation for giving his bread to a very big prisoner who found it impossible to live on prison rations. One of the prisoners, Willie Corrigan, complained about the thin gruel. 'I will look into it,' the prison doctor promised. 'If you look into it,' Corrigan told the doctor, 'you will see the bottom of the mug.' The water was heavy with iron and the prisoners' teeth began to rot.

The other group of convicted prisoners were sent to Portland in Dorset, where they found a long, narrow causeway jutting out into the English Channel. Here, a grim Victorian fortress stood on a rocky promontory. The guards carried shotguns and short swords. At this prison the most dangerous prisoners in England were held—murderers, rapists and escapers. They had been sentenced to hard labour and were taken out each day, rain or snow, chained to a wagon and marched to the quarries, where they cut stone. The prisoners from Ireland had been sentenced to penal servitude, which meant that they avoided the backbreaking labour in the quarries. They were issued with 'blue striped shirts and brown knee breeches' and a jacket stamped with arrows. Prisoners were called by their number and never by their name. The men were put to work sewing mail sacks or 'picking oakum'. Dinner was a pint of cocoa, a twelve-ounce loaf and

half an ounce of margarine. The men were in bed by 8pm each night. Spells of isolation with bread and water were meted out for minor infractions. Prisoners who assaulted warders were lashed with 'the cat' but none of the Irish prisoners were punished in that way and it seems that they fared rather better than others. They had access to books and a chaplain, and medical treatment was adequate.

The first batch of prisoners interned without trial were released in August 1916; the rest were released just before Christmas. The reasons for the release of the internees were complex. The legality of their continued detention was questionable. Asquith's government favoured conciliation and the tide of opinion in Ireland had turned in favour of the prisoners. There was also an international dimension: the government at Westminster needed America to enter the war and conciliation of Irish-American opinion was part of this complex diplomatic manoeuvring. The convicted prisoners would be held until June 1917.

Seán Enright is the author of After the Rising: soldiers, lawyers and trials of the Irish Revolution *(Merrion Press, 2016).*

●
Above: Prisoners under guard in Richmond Barracks in 1916. (NLI)

●
Opposite page: A group of prisoners in Frongoch camp in Wales in the aftermath of the Easter Rising. (NLI)

The women of Cumann na mBan '... went to work with a right good will on the Fund, the success of which was much greater than we had anticipated'.

THE PRISONERS' DEPENDANTS' FUND

BY **LIZ GILLIS**

In the immediate aftermath of the Rising, with most of the male leadership either dead or in prison, women came to the fore in the movement in support of prisoners and their families. Kathleen Clarke, widow of Tom Clarke, first signatory of the Proclamation of the Irish Republic, was given £3,000 by the Irish Republican Brotherhood (IRB) to help the families of those rebels who had died or were in prison. Each commandant of the Irish Volunteers had made lists of the dependants of their men, but these and other such documents were destroyed to prevent their discovery as the British military raided the houses of known republicans. Clarke, aided by Sorcha MacMahon of central branch, Cumann na mBan, had to start from scratch to locate those who needed help. So was begun the Irish Republican Prisoners' Dependants' Fund, later known as the Irish Volunteers' Dependants' Fund. At the same time another relief organisation had been set up—the National Aid Association. This differed from the Dependants' Fund in

●

Above: Members of the Irish Citizen Army pictured with their families outside the ruins of Liberty Hall after the Easter Rising. (NLI)

that it had a large committee; the Dependants' Fund committee only had three members. In addition, National Aid was made up of people from across the political spectrum, including the Irish Parliamentary Party (IPP) and Cumann na mBan. Both organisations had difficulty at first in getting information from relatives, who were reluctant to come forward for fear of arrest. Both organisations also realised that they would need large amounts of money to provide relief for all those who needed it. Somehow funds would have to be raised.

Kathleen Clarke had come up with the idea of holding a series of flag days, one every Sunday in memory of the executed leaders, in order to raise money. She was prevented from doing so by General Sir John Maxwell, who sent her a letter stating that anyone involved in such activities would be arrested under the Defence of the Realm Act for 'causing disaffection to His Majesty the King'.

Something, however, needed to be done. The people of Ireland had to know that the Rising was not an isolated event. It fell to the women of Cumann na mBan and the Irish Citizen Army (ICA) to spread that message. The British were well trained in the art of propaganda but, much to their surprise, so too were the women. Within weeks of the executions, Cumann na mBan organised a Mass to be said in memory of those who had died. This was only the beginning.

With both relief organisations working for the same goal, the most logical step was amalgamation. Kathleen Clarke refused, as she felt that National Aid was controlled by the IPP, who would use it to further their political agenda. After much

●

Right: Kathleen Clarke (née Daly), the widow of Thomas J. Clarke, and their three sons, John Daly Clarke, Tom Clarke and Emmet Clarke, pictured after the Easter Rising. Her husband had been one of the key figures in the planning of the Rising; she in turn became a prime mover in the establishment of welfare organisations for prisoners and their families in the aftermath. This image of a family in mourning was widely used for fund-raising purposes. (NLI)

negotiation, helped by the efforts of Cumann na mBan, the two organisations amalgamated and became the National Aid and Volunteers' Dependants' Fund (NADVF). Pooling their resources, they continued their work in earnest. Distribution committees were set up throughout the country. In Dublin, each branch of Cumann na mBan collected in their locality. After a day's work, they would go collecting through their neighbourhoods. Every week they would then go around the city distributing the money. As Clarke herself said, the women of Cumann na mBan '... went to work with a

right good will on the Fund, the success of which was much greater than we had anticipated'. In the chaos that followed the Rising many families did not know whether their loved ones had been killed or were in prison, and the NADVF was inundated with requests for information. Lily O'Brennan, sister-in-law of Éamonn Ceannt, and Anno O'Rahilly, sister of The O'Rahilly, undertook this work and went around the cemeteries trying to locate the graves of Volunteers. On finding a grave they would mark it with a small iron cross.

Cumann na mBan's work was

not just confined to Ireland. Clan na Gael, the American wing of the republican movement, which had helped to fund the Rising, was eager to hear what had really happened. As most IRB men were in prison or on the run, this job was given to Cumann na mBan. Alice Cashel and Min Ryan, who had both been involved in Easter Week, were amongst those chosen to go to America and report on the events. Their journeys were far from easy, as Cashel later explained: 'Before

● Above: A catalogue for a fund-raising auction for the INAVDF in Dublin's Mansion House, April 1918. Amongst the more notable items on sale were Robert Emmet's wallet and the block on which he was allegedly beheaded, along with blank canvasses provided by the artists John Lavery and William Orpen, on which they offered to paint portraits of the highest bidder. (Courtesy of Kilmainham Gaol Museum 18BK-1K55-09)

● Opposite page: Jubilant crowds waving tri-colours on the platform at Westland Row greet a train carrying released republican prisoners. Having been detained after the Rising, all of the prisoners were freed by June 1917. (NLI)

embarking we were sent one by one before a [British] military investigation council and closely questioned'. Despite the previous threat of arrest from General Maxwell, the women were determined to continue their work for the NADVF. As well as collecting in their own areas, they would also collect outside churches all over the country. Eilís Ní Riain, central branch, Cumann na mBan, remembered noticing the change in public opinion through these collections:

'... people who had refused to subscribe before now gave generously and sympathetically. This gave us great courage and resulted in filling several boxes on Sundays instead of merely one.'

And the women would definitely need that courage, as there is no doubt that this work did not go unnoticed by the police; as time went on, many of the women were to be arrested for such activities. As well as providing relief for the families of the Volunteers, the Dependants' Fund also sent relief to the men who were interned. Women such as Muriel MacSwiney were sent over to England with parcels for the men and also to find out from them what was happening in the prisons and internment camps. Despite the best efforts of the authorities to censor letters and correspondence, the men got word to the women, who in turn reported their findings back in Ireland.

With public opinion now favouring the Volunteers and mounting pressure from political bodies, the British government decided to release those interned in Frongoch. They returned home to Ireland on Christmas Eve 1916, but many were unable to continue their journey home to their towns and villages. Again the Dependants' Fund was on hand to help, ensuring that everyone was housed in and around Dublin city and that they were well cared for. The reaction from the public must have been a shock to the men. Only seven months earlier they had been jeered and attacked and now they were heroes. And this

homecoming was in no small part due to the hard work of Cumann na mBan.

One Volunteer amongst those returning was Michael Collins, who, although unknown in 1916, would quickly rise to prominence in republican circles. He contacted Kathleen Clarke and she was impressed by this young man, who reminded her of Seán MacDiarmada. With her support he was appointed secretary of the Dependants' Fund. A keen organiser, he used the cover of his position with the Fund to help with the reorganisation of the Volunteers and, more importantly, the IRB.

Reorganisation of the Volunteers, Na Fianna and Cumann na mBan was now intensified. Membership of Cumann na mBan increased dramatically, with at least 100 branches in existence in 1917; this would increase to 500 in 1918. In February 1917 the North Roscommon by-election showed just how much public opinion had changed. Although standing as an independent candidate, Count Plunkett, whose son Joseph was executed after the Rising, won the seat. Cumann na mBan played their part in securing this victory. According to Eilís Ní Riain, she and her comrades volunteered at the campaign office. There they typed circulars, addressed envelopes and did whatever else was necessary. The election of Count Plunkett was an enormous coup for the republican movement, as Plunkett had stood against IPP member Thomas Devine. On the suggestion of Michael Collins, it was decided that Volunteer Joseph McGuinness should stand for Sinn Féin in the next by-election in Longford in May 1917. McGuinness was still in prison in England for his part in the Rising. This did not deter the campaigners, including Cumann na mBan, who canvassed the towns and villages, drumming up support for their candidate. Their efforts were rewarded when McGuinness narrowly beat the IPP candidate, Patrick McKenna.

Always aware of the importance of propaganda, the women continued in their work. On the first anniver-

sary of the Rising the ICA women posted reprints of the Proclamation all over Dublin city. On the anniversary of the execution of James Connolly, on the suggestion of Helena Molony, a large banner with the words 'James Connolly Murdered May 12th 1916' was hung across the shell of Liberty Hall. It was quickly removed by the police. A new one was made and Molony, Brigid Davis, Rosie Hackett and Jinny Shanahan went to the roof of Liberty Hall, barricaded the door and unfurled the banner. It took nearly 400 policemen four hours to break through and remove the banner.

Realising that the political climate was changing in Ireland and in order to regain some control, the British government announced the release of prisoners incarcerated in England. Although the majority, including de Valera, came home on 20 June 1917, there was no sign of Countess Markievicz. She was due to arrive the following day and, when she did, thousands were there to welcome her home, including her comrades of the ICA and Cumann na mBan. During her imprisonment she had been elected president of Cumann na mBan, and after a few days' rest she returned to her revolutionary activities.

An important point to note is that, although everyone was released by mid-1917 and there was a lot of hostility towards the authorities, the republicans did *not* take up arms. Over the next two and a half years their policy was one of civil disobedience and making their case for independence through political means. Despite this, the British government continued with its coercive behaviour, banning meetings and eventually declaring all republican bodies, including Cumann na mBan, illegal organisations.

Liz Gillis is author of May 25: burning of the Custom House 1921 *(Kilmainham Tales Publications, 2017).*

Further reading

L. Conlon, *Cumann na mBan and the women of Ireland 1913–25* (Kilkenny, 1969).

L. Gillis, *Women of the Irish Revolution* (Cork, 2014).

H. Litton, *Kathleen Clarke: revolutionary woman* (Dublin, 2008).

M. Ward, *Unmanageable revolutionaries: women and Irish nationalism* (London, 1983).

LIFE IN FRONGOCH

BY JOSEPH E.A. CONNELL JR

Frongoch internment camp was located in a former whiskey distillery in Merionethshire, Wales. Until 1916 it housed German prisoners of war in the disused distillery buildings and crude huts, but in the wake of the Rising the German prisoners were moved and it was used as a place of internment for approximately 1,800 Irish prisoners. They were accorded POW status.

Joe Clarke, who had served in the 3rd Battalion in the Rising and was posted to Clanwilliam House at Mount Street Bridge, recalled:

'After the Battle of Mount Street Bridge I was arrested and kept in military barracks in Dublin for about ten days when we were taken to the North Wall and put aboard a cattle boat and taken to Wakefield Jail in Yorkshire. We were in solitary confinement there for about three weeks and late in the month of May 1916 we were transferred to Frongoch camp in Wales. This camp was formerly occupied by German prisoners as their names were written in the German language on the walls. We had between 900 and 1,000 prisoners about the middle of June. We were all brought in batches every other day to Wandsworth Jail where we spent two nights. We were then questioned by an Advisory Committee about our actions in Ireland about the Rising. A big number of us refused to answer any questions and following that, about the middle of July, half of the prisoners were released in batches every other day. Between four and five hundred, including myself, were detained until the 23rd of December when we were released.'

Because so many of the prisoners had received some military training leading up to the Rising, they soon established a military command structure. The camp became fertile ground for the spreading of the revolutionary gospel, and later became known as the 'University of Revolution' or the 'Sinn Féin University'.

A look at the names of just a few of those who were imprisoned in Frongoch gives an idea of the 'talent' that was available to teach and inspire the men to follow the revolutionary doctrine. Capt. Michael Collins was Prisoner 1320 here. Paddy Daly went on hunger strike after being punished for a minor infraction of the camp rules. The strike was successful. Later he became a major-general in the Irish Army. Capt. Leo Henderson became O/C in charge of the 1st Dormitory. He later organised the 'Belfast Boycott', and was arrested in a raid on Ferguson's Garage at the start of the Civil War. The King brothers (Arthur, George, Michael and Sam) were taken from Frongoch and handed over to the British military for desertion; they were eventually discharged as 'persons not likely to give loyal and faithful service to His Majesty'. Brian O'Higgins was one of the party who moved the explosives into the GPO basement. He was imprisoned in Frongoch, became a TD and fought on the anti-Treaty side in the Civil War. He wrote *The soldier's story of Easter Week*. Capt. Michael W. O'Reilly was the Camp O/C at Frongoch and subsequently was Director of Training for the IRA.

Joseph E.A. Connell Jr is the author of Michael Collins: Dublin 1916–22 *(Wordwell Books).*

Further reading

L. Ebenezer, *Fron-Goch and the birth of the IRA* (Conwy, 2005).

S. O'Mahony, *Frongoch, University of Revolution* (Dublin, 1987).

S. Ó Maoileoin, *B'fhiu an Braon Fola* (Baile Átha Cliath, 1958).

This article first appeared in the 'Countdown to 2016' series in HI 24.5, Sept./Oct. 2016.

Below: A line-drawing by an artist known only as 'McD' of the North Camp at Frongoch in Wales in 1916. (NLI)

A TURNING TIDE

'The conscription crisis contributed greatly to the extent of Sinn Féin's crushing defeat of the Irish Party in the general election of December 1918, but a close analysis of the by-elections that preceded that vote show how crucial they were in building post-Rising Sinn Féin up to the level where it could pose such a threat to the party which had dominated Irish nationalist politics for most of the previous 50 years.'

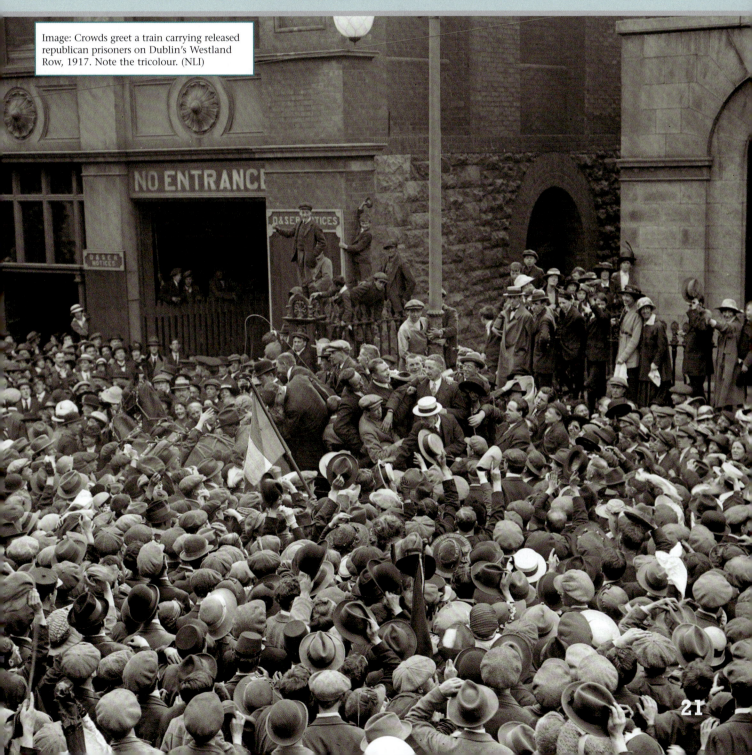

Image: Crowds greet a train carrying released republican prisoners on Dublin's Westland Row, 1917. Note the tricolour. (NLI)

'The Irish Party
Wounded in North Roscommon
Killed in South Longford
Buried in East Clare
R.I.P.'

THE 1917 BY-ELECTIONS AND THE RISE OF SINN FÉIN

BY **MARIE COLEMAN**

A flag erected outside Birr Castle in King's County (Offaly) in mid-1917 neatly summed up the impact of a series of by-elections in altering the political landscape of nationalist Ireland just over a year after the Easter Rising. These electoral contests were crucial to the process whereby the resurgent post-Rising Sinn Féin emerged to replace the old Home Rule party as the principal political representative of nationalist Ireland between the Rising and the 1918 general election.

As early as 11 May 1916, a day before the executions of Seán MacDiarmada and James Connolly, John Dillon warned the British government in a perceptive speech in the House of Commons that the executions were 'poisoning the mind of Ireland'. The harshness of the British response to the Rising and the inaccurate attribution of it to Sinn Féin rescued that party from relative obscurity before the Rising, when it was a small, largely Dublin-based radical grouping whose only notable public representative was W.T. Cosgrave on Dublin Corporation.

The abortive Home Rule negotiations during the summer of 1916 dealt a further blow to the credibility of Redmond and the Irish Party. During these negotiations Redmond had made a significant concession on partition that alienated many Ulster nationalists, who formed the breakaway Irish Nation League, which would eventually merge with Sinn Féin. When the negotiations failed owing to the duplicity of the government's chief negotiator—the minister for munitions, David Lloyd George—and the recalcitrance of the southern unionists, Redmond was left in a position of having effectively traded partition and gained nothing in return. He had failed in his last opportunity of achieving Irish Home Rule, and in the process lost an important sector of his party's supporters.

In spite of these setbacks, at the outset of 1917 the IPP remained the largest representative of nationalist Ireland, nationally and locally. In many ways it became a victim of bad luck owing to an unusually high number of by-elections occurring in a short space of time; ten parliamentary vacancies arose that year, the highest number in any one year between the general elections of 1910 and 1918. Six of these were occasioned by the deaths of sitting members. With the exception of Major Willie Redmond in East Clare, all of the Irish Party MPs whose deaths led to the vacancies were in their 60s and 70s: Patrick O'Kelly in North Roscommon was 71, John Phillips (South Longford) was 77 and Patrick O'Brien (Kilkenny City) was 64. All three died of natural causes resulting from ill health.

The 1911 Parliament Act had reduced the maximum lifespan of parliament from seven to five years, so that following the two elections in 1910 the next election was due to be held in 1915, but this was postponed because of the war. As a consequence, a number of these older IPP MPs who might well have retired at that point remained in place. Thus the party lost the opportunity to inject new blood into its parliamentary representation and a number of its older members died at an electorally inconvenient moment.

The first of these vacancies arose in February 1917 in the western constituency of North Roscommon following the death of the old Fenian O'Kelly, who had been first elected to parliament for Roscommon as a Land League candidate in 1880 (losing his seat briefly between 1892 and 1895 after taking the Parnellite side in the split). George Noble Count Plunkett, father of the executed 1916 rebel Joseph Mary Plunkett, was put forward to contest the by-election, though not officially as a Sinn Féin candidate, and he enjoyed a comfortable victory over the IPP's T.J. Devine, polling 3,022 votes to the latter's 1,708.

As Michael Laffan has shown, the extent of Plunkett's victory owed much to his status as the father of an executed rebel and the particular circumstances of County Roscommon, where there had been a large number of arrests after the Rising and where a strong Sinn Féin organisation had been put in place by Fr Michael O'Flanagan. By contrast, the Home Rule organisation

was weak and riven by internal conflict; the cantankerous editor of the *Roscommon Herald* newspaper, Jasper Tully, contested the by-election as an independent nationalist but only polled 687 votes. Plunkett's winning margin was still greater than the combined nationalist and independent nationalist vote.

Internal divisions in the Home Rule movement also contributed significantly to the IPP's defeat in the next by-election, which took place in May 1917 in the neighbouring constituency of South Longford. John Redmond was forced to impose a candidate after three nationalists sought the nomination. Consequently, supporters of the two unsuccessful candidates refused to back Redmond's choice of Patrick McKenna.

Buoyed by their success in Roscommon, Sinn Féin supporters approached a 1916 internee, Joseph McGuinness, who had lived in the county previously. In spite of much opposition from his fellow 1916 inmates in Lewes prison, McGuinness was nominated, winning the seat by a slim margin of 37 votes after a tense recount. The intervention of the Catholic archbishop of Dublin, William Walsh, in support of him on the eve of the poll was a decisive factor in his success, as was the level of decline which had taken hold of the local IPP organisation, the United Irish League, in the county since before the First World War. Among the prominent local defectors from the UIL to Sinn Féin was the candidate's brother, Frank McGuinness, a prominent businessman in Longford town.

The death in June 1917 of Major Willie Redmond from wounds suffered while fighting with the army in Belgium led to the next vacancy, in East Clare. This was the first by-election to take place after the release of the remaining 1916 prisoners in June, and the most prominent of these, Éamon de Valera, won the election for Sinn Féin, gaining over 70% of the votes cast. The loss of the seat that had been held by John Redmond's brother since 1892 to the new leader of nationalist Ireland was a significant symbolic defeat for the Irish Party. Sinn Féin completed its successful electoral sweep in 1917 when W.T. Cosgrave won the Kilkenny City by-election in August. In line with stated Sinn Féin policy, all of the MPs elected in 1917 abstained from the Westminster parliament.

In three of these constituencies there had not been a contested election since 1895, and since 1892 in the case of Longford, with the result that the Irish Party was unprepared

●

Above: De Valera speaking to a crowd of well-wishers after his victory in the 1917 East Clare by-election, occasioned by the death of Willie Redmond in Ypres. (NLI)

IRELAND AT THE CROSS-ROADS.

LYNCH
THE SHAM CONVENTION
HUMBUG &

DE VALERA,
THE
PEACE CONFERENCE &

FREEDOM

SHAM

HUMBUG

CONVENTION

FOREIGN RULE

TAXATION

VOTE FOR **DE VALERA** And the Road to Freedom.

Above: Cartoon from the 1917 East Clare by-election depicting Ireland at a cross-roads, making the choice either of sitting at the post-war Peace Conference or of following the IPP candidate Patrick Lynch down a road characterised by taxation and foreign rule. (NLI)

for facing electoral competition. This, along with the relative cessation of land agitation, contributed to a prolonged weakening of the structures of the party's local organisation, the United Irish League.

The status of three of the candidates as 1916 rebels, and of the fourth as the father of an executed leader of the rebellion, was a significant factor in attracting support for the Sinn Féin candidates. In the Longford contest the slogan of 'Put him in to get him out' raised awareness of the campaign for an amnesty for the 1916 internees, which was eventually granted in June. Yet the Rising alone does not explain the extent of Sinn Féin's electoral success in 1917; the progress of the war was equally important.

A doggerel verse quoted in the *Roscommon Herald* during the Longford contest proclaimed of the Irish Party that:

They gave their benediction
To an Ireland cut in two
They would glorify conscription
If their lease they would renew.

After 1914 it was clear that at least part of Ulster would be excluded in some form from Home Rule when it came into effect. The damage done to the Irish Party by Redmond's post-Rising acquiescence to a parti-

tionist solution became clear during the Longford by-election when Archbishop Walsh of Dublin wrote a letter to the national evening newspapers on the eve of the election lamenting 'that the mischief has already been done and that the country is practically sold'.

Conscription had particular resonance in rural constituencies, such as Longford, Roscommon and Clare, where Irish farmers were benefiting from the wartime economy and fearful of the prospect that their sons would be forced to join the army. While Ireland had been exempted from compulsory military service in 1916, casualty figures continued to rise and the threat of its extension loomed. During the by-elections, and especially in the Longford contest, Sinn Féin was successful in convincing voters that it was the only party that could defend Ireland from conscription. Although opposed to compulsory military service, the IPP was tainted by its support for voluntary recruitment and Sinn Féin effectively blurred the distinction between both.

The significance of the by-elections in rejuvenating Sinn Féin at local level in areas where the by-elections took place is clear from the fact that by the end of 1917 three of the four counties where the party enjoyed its strongest membership proportionate to the counties' population had been the location for these contests—Clare, Longford and Roscommon.

Nationally, this series of by-election victories forged Sinn Féin into a cohesive political party. At the start of 1917 it was still a loose coalition of advanced nationalists, and many republicans were still wary of Griffith's earlier support for a dual monarchy. After the Roscommon contest there was considerable confusion over the status of Count Plunkett's Liberty League. Much had changed by the time Sinn Féin held its first *ard fheis* in October 1917, at which de Valera was elected president and the pledge to achieve an 'independent Irish Republic' was adopted.

The demise of Irish Party MPs continued into 1918 with the deaths

THE
IRISH PARTY'S
Only Props
IN LONGFORD

Sinn Féin's crushing defeat of the Irish Party in the general election of December 1918, but a close analysis of the by-elections that preceded that vote show how crucial they were in building post-Rising Sinn Féin up to the level where it could pose such a threat to the party which had dominated Irish nationalist politics for most of the previous 50 years.

Marie Coleman is Senior Lecturer in Irish History at the School of History, Anthropology, Philosophy and Politics, Queen's University Belfast.

Further reading

M. Coleman, *County Longford and the Irish Revolution, 1910–1923* (Dublin, 2003).

M. Coleman, *The Irish Revolution, 1916–1923* (London, 2013).

M. Laffan, *The resurrection of Ireland: the Sinn Féin Party, 1916–1923* (Cambridge, 1999).

C. Mulvagh, *The Irish Parliamentary Party at Westminster, 1900–1918* (Manchester, 2016).

●

Left: Sinn Féin election material from the 1917 South Longford by-election in which Joseph McGuinness beat the IPP candidate. (NLI)

●

Below: Joseph McGuinness (1875–1922) won his seat in the South Longford by-election in 1917 while in prison for his involvement in the Easter Rising. (NLI)

IRISH REPUBLICAN ARMY. 1916.

JOSEPH McGUINNESS,
(Sentenced to 3 years imprisonment)
ELECTED FOR SOUTH LONGFORD, MAY, 1917.

of Dr Charles O'Neill in January (aged 69) and the party leader John Redmond (aged 61) in February. The party recovered slightly from its 1917 experience, regaining both seats in South Armagh and Waterford, and a third in East Tyrone occasioned by the resignation of Redmond's son, Captain William Archer Redmond, following his election to his father's old seat in Waterford.

Any sense that these victories represented a serious recovery was illusory, however. Two of the seats had strong Redmond connections, so it was hardly surprising that the party retained them. Two were in Ulster, where the IPP's principal local organisation was the Ancient Order of Hibernians and displayed a greater resilience than the UIL in the south, partly because of the existence of political competition from unionists. In South Armagh the IPP candidate, Patrick Donnelly, was a well-known local solicitor, whereas Patrick McCartan was a blow-in originally from Tyrone who had spent many years in the USA, and the local unionist electorate either abstained or appear to have given some support to Donnelly.

Any nascent recovery by the Irish Party was doomed by the government's fateful decision to attempt to extend conscription to Ireland in March 1918. The conscription crisis contributed greatly to the extent of

The Firing Party At The Grave Of Thomas Ashe, September, 30, 1917.

If the funeral of Jeremiah O'Donovan Rossa in 1915 was the 'pilot' for the 1916 Rising, Thomas Ashe's on 30 September 1917 was the sequel.

THE FUNERAL OF THOMAS ASHE

BY **JOHN GIBNEY**

Just before 2pm on Sunday 30 September 1917, Thomas Ashe made his final journey from Dublin's City Hall to Glasnevin Cemetery. The enormous procession that left City Hall followed what had become a well-worn pattern for political funerals going to Glasnevin, and the funeral of Ashe was nothing if not politicised; indeed, the departure had been advertised to take place at 1.30pm, thereby ignoring the unpopular abolition of the 35-minute difference between 'Dublin Mean Time' and 'Greenwich Mean Time' in favour of the latter the previous year—a small form of symbolic resistance to the British government that had made the change. In the days prior to the funeral thousands had filed past Ashe's coffin, which had lain in state, guarded by members of the Irish Volunteers, in the rotunda of City Hall. The funeral itself was organised by the 'Wolfe Tone Memorial Committee'; this was a flag of convenience for the Irish Republican Brotherhood, of which Ashe had been a leading member and which had previously been used to organise the funeral of Jeremiah O'Donovan Rossa in August 1915. The committee, reformed for the occasion, sought the use of City Hall for Ashe's funeral from Lord Mayor Laurence O'Neill in the face of pressure from the British authorities. The prospect of confrontation was defused after O'Neill and the new Sinn Féin MP for Kilkenny, veteran Dublin alderman W.T. Cosgrave, interceded with Lt General Sir Bryan Mahon, the incumbent general officer commanding in Ireland.

Mahon, an Irish-born veteran of the Gallipoli campaign, had replaced Sir John Maxwell the previous year in a move that was assumed to mark a departure from his predecessor's heavy-handedness; Mahon ignored orders from Dublin Castle to restrict any overt displays of republican militarism and kept his forces out of the way of the funeral arrangements.

This was no ordinary funeral. If O'Donovan Rossa's funeral had served as a milestone on the road to the Easter Rising, that of Ashe was to be a milestone, in symbolic and actual terms, in the development of the independence movement that came to prominence after the Rising. Yet it could also be seen as a blow to that same movement, marking as it did the death of a figure who had seemed destined for a major leadership role. Ashe was originally from Lispole, in the Kerry Gaeltacht. He joined the Gaelic League while at school and later trained as a teacher, becoming master of Corduff national school near Lusk in County Dublin. He was sympathetic to the cause of labour, and was involved in a wide range of cultural and political organisations, being a talented piper and a member of the GAA. At some point he had joined the IRB and, in 1913, the Irish Volunteers. Ashe commanded the Volunteers in Fingal, in north County Dublin, and during the Easter Rising led his battalion to disrupt communications and transport infrastructure both there and in Meath. They were responsible for the most notable and successful incident of the Rising outside Dublin, when they defeated a substantial RIC force at Ashbourne and captured the local police barracks after a five-hour gun battle involving the use of guerilla tactics.

Ashe was sentenced to death after the Rising but the sentence was commuted and he was imprisoned in Dartmoor and Lewes, where his role in Easter Week secured his stature amongst his fellow republican prisoners; he was released in the general amnesty of June 1917 and resumed his activism. He became president of the supreme council of the IRB, helping to revise its constitution, and campaigned for Éamon de Valera (with whom he had been imprisoned in Lewes) in the East Clare by-election caused by the death of the sitting Home Rule MP, Willie Redmond, who had been killed at the Battle of Messines. After giving a 'seditious' speech in Longford later that summer, Ashe was arrested under the wartime Defence of the Realm Act and received a two-year prison sentence for his trouble. He was imprisoned in Mountjoy Prison and was one of 40 prisoners who went on hunger strike on 20 September, demanding to be recognised as prisoners of war. The hunger strikers were force-fed: they were strapped into a chair and a mixture of raw eggs beaten in milk was pumped into their stomach through a tube inserted through the nose or mouth. Ashe was force-fed for the first time on 23 September. Two days later he was force-fed by an inexperienced doctor, seemingly with considerable force; the feeding tube entered his lung and he immediately became ill. Ashe died on the evening of 25 September in the Mater Hospital, after his lungs filled with fluid.

The circumstances of Ashe's death had a powerful resonance in the context of the shifting currents of Irish political life in the wake of the Easter Rising; here, it seemed fair to say, was another victim of British repression. On the day of his death crowds had gathered outside the Mater and Mountjoy. The opportunity to capitalise on such an emotive event was not lost on the IRB; they organised the funeral, and the Irish National Aid and Volunteers' Dependants' Fund paid the costs. Ashe's funeral Mass was celebrated in the Pro-Cathedral before the coffin was transferred to City Hall, as the first act of the elaborate political theatre that took place on the streets of Dublin on Sunday 30 September 1917.

Ashe's funeral was a massive event; the *Irish Times* dubbed it 'a great Sinn Féin demonstration', while also noting that 'the funeral was the largest which had been seen in Dublin since that of Mr Parnell'. Crowds had gathered in the city from midday, with republican

●

Opposite page: A postcard depicting members of the 'Dublin Brigade of the Irish Republican Army' forming the firing party over Ashe's grave in Glasnevin Cemetery. Three volleys of shots were followed by Michael Collins's short, if militant, oration. (Kilmainham Gaol Museum)

●

Below: Memorial wreaths adorn Ashe's grave in Glasnevin Cemetery, with the O'Connell Tower in the background. His grave was located in the area that would evolve into the Republican Plot, and was directly behind that of Jeremiah O'Donovan Rossa. (Capuchin Archives)

"Ceaσuiξ σam, a Ṫiaṗna,
σo Ċṗoiṡ σ'iomċaṗ ṫaṗ
cionn na héiṗeann.

Above: A memorial card for Thomas Ashe; there was a brisk trade in such souvenirs on the day of the funeral and afterwards. (Glasnevin Trust)

range of organisations, including both the Irish Volunteers and the National Volunteers, the Black Raven Pipe Band (which Ashe had helped to found in Lusk), Sinn Féin, Cumann na mBan, the Irish Women's Franchise League, a vast range of unions (though, it being Sunday, not bakers), a large contingent of teachers, Dublin Fire Brigade and members of the GAA with hurleys (the Dublin County Board condemned the death of a member and the association was heavily represented in the procession), while Dublin Corporation workers contributed a truck adorned with an 8ft-high Celtic cross made of flowers. The cortège took 90 minutes to get to Glasnevin, having taken a route established by previous Fenian funerals: Lord Edward Street, High Street, Thomas Street (the site of the execution of Robert Emmet), Bridgefoot Street, the North Quays, Sackville (O'Connell) Street and Phibsborough. According to the *Evening Herald*, the procession was three miles long and 30,000 strong; the rearguard was apparently still passing City Hall even as the funeral arrived in Glasnevin later that afternoon. Trams were suspended, church bells tolled along the route and the sobriety of the crowds was noted; even the *Times* acknowledged that it was 'orderly'. The Irish Volunteers and Na Fianna Éireann took advantage of the hands-off stance of the British Army and marshalled the funeral route from City Hall. Some colourful details were recorded: youths were seen using the elephant over Elvery's in Sackville Street as a vantage point, the Orange Hall on Parnell Square was notably unadorned, while the shop on the North Circular Road owned by the O'Hanrahans—the family of the executed 1916 leader Michael O'Hanrahan—was draped in black. The Volunteers called 'eyes right' while passing the Mater Hospital, to acknowledge some of Ashe's fellow prisoners there, while *The Soldier's Song* was played outside Mountjoy Prison itself. The cortège arrived at Glasnevin by 3.45pm (Ashe's funeral was the last of seven

insignia and black armbands being widely worn and vendors doing a good trade in memorial cards. Members of the Irish Volunteers carried the coffin out of City Hall, draped in a tricolour, and the

cortège was led by Catholic clergy; in a major departure from the Catholic Church's traditional stance towards the Fenians, the archbishop of Dublin, William Walsh, condemned the treatment of Ashe and was represented in the procession, which he viewed from the presbytery on Arran Quay. The clergy were followed by the hearse, the Ashe family, the lord mayor and a diverse

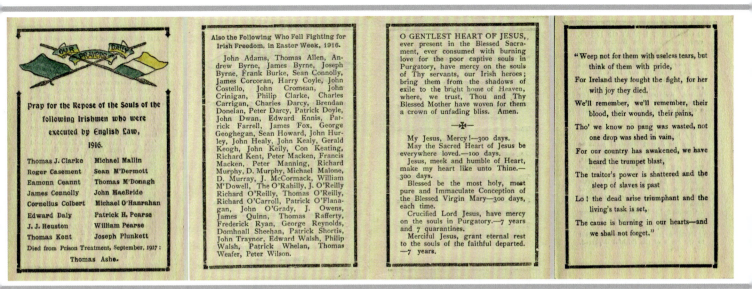

held that day). The Volunteers cordoned off the cemetery and, after a service in the chapel, Ashe was buried adjacent to James Stephens, John O'Leary and O'Donovan Rossa in the area that would eventually evolve into the 'Republican plot'. Three volleys were fired by a party from what was apparently described as the 'Dublin Brigade of the Irish Republican Army'. After the firing party had concluded, Michael Collins—a relatively unknown figure in public at this juncture—gave an exceptionally short oration in Irish and English: 'Nothing additional remains to be said. That volley which we have just heard is the only speech it is proper to make over the grave of a dead Fenian.' Crowds continued to arrive even after the funeral party departed. The last contingent had left by 6.30pm, and by 10pm newsreels of the funeral were being shown in the Bohemian Cinema in Phibsborough, a short distance from where Ashe had been laid to rest.

● Above: Another memorial card for Ashe, explicitly recruiting him into the ranks of the fallen of Easter Week. (Capuchin Archives)

● Right: Fr Albert Bibby, Fr J.F. Sweetman and Fr Augustine Hayden take part in the funeral cortège of Thomas Ashe. Capuchin friars, including Frs Albert and Augustine, had ministered at the executions of the 1916 leaders in Kilmainham Gaol; both clerics had attended to Ashe as he lay dying in Dublin's Mater Hospital. (Capuchin Archives)

The significance of Thomas Ashe's funeral was not lost on observers, including the British authorities. John Dillon, in parliament, claimed that 'Ashe, by his death, had done more for Sinn Féin, and brought more recruits to their ranks, then if he lived for a thousand years'. It is tempting to speculate on what such an energetic and intensely practical figure would have achieved had he lived; Ashe's stature within the separatist movement, in the summer of 1917, was apparently on a par with that of de Valera. Yet even aside from the political impact of his death, his funeral provided a more practical opportunity around

which the Irish Volunteers, many of whom had come from all across Ireland, could mobilise. After the Rising many (if not most) of the Volunteer leadership were dead or imprisoned. A new, temporary Volunteer executive had been established in Dublin under the stewardship of Cathal Brugha in late 1916–17, and the process of reorganising the Volunteers had been taking place at local level in some areas. In May 1917 Volunteers were ordered to prioritise involvement in their own organisation above that of others, which may indicate that in the fluid circumstances of 1917 their attention and energies could be

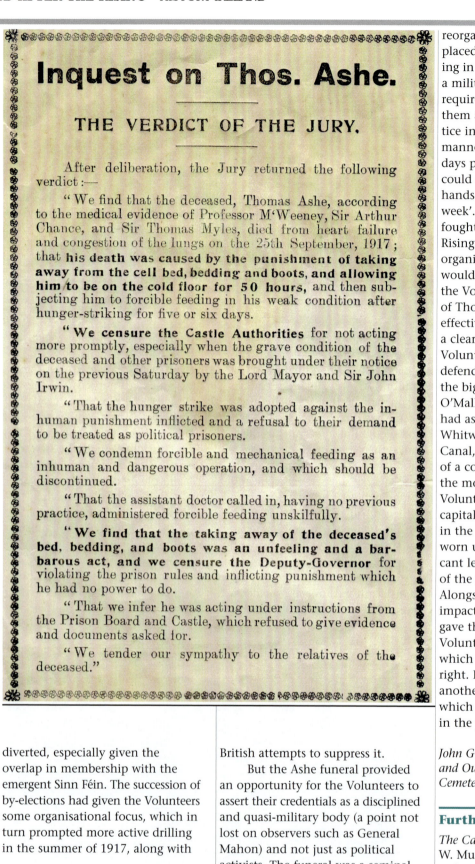

Inquest on Thos. Ashe.

THE VERDICT OF THE JURY.

After deliberation, the Jury returned the following verdict :—

"We find that the deceased, Thomas Ashe, according to the medical evidence of Professor M'Weeney, Sir Arthur Chance, and Sir Thomas Myles, died from heart failure and congestion of the lungs on the 25th September, 1917; **that his death was caused by the punishment of taking away from the cell bed, bedding and boots, and allowing him to be on the cold floor for 50 hours,** and then subjecting him to forcible feeding in his weak condition after hunger-striking for five or six days.

"**We censure the Castle Authorities** for not acting more promptly, especially when the grave condition of the deceased and other prisoners was brought under their notice on the previous Saturday by the Lord Mayor and Sir John Irwin.

"That the hunger strike was adopted against the in-human punishment inflicted and a refusal to their demand to be treated as political prisoners.

"We condemn forcible and mechanical feeding as an inhuman and dangerous operation, and which should be discontinued.

"That the assistant doctor called in, having no previous practice, administered forcible feeding unskilfully.

"**We find that the taking away of the deceased's bed, bedding, and boots was an unfeeling and a barbarous act, and we censure the Deputy-Governor** for violating the prison rules and inflicting punishment which he had no power to do.

"That we infer he was acting under instructions from the Prison Board and Castle, which refused to give evidence and documents asked for.

"We tender our sympathy to the relatives of the deceased."

Above: A pamphlet highlighting the findings of the inquest into Ashe's death, which gave an enormous propaganda boost to republicans; the veteran barrister and Home Rule MP Tim Healy had represented the Ashe family. (Glasnevin Trust)

diverted, especially given the overlap in membership with the emergent Sinn Féin. The succession of by-elections had given the Volunteers some organisational focus, which in turn prompted more active drilling in the summer of 1917, along with

British attempts to suppress it.

But the Ashe funeral provided an opportunity for the Volunteers to assert their credentials as a disciplined and quasi-military body (a point not lost on observers such as General Mahon) and not just as political activists. The funeral was a seminal moment not only in terms of the shift in Irish public opinion towards supporting the separatism of the Rising but also in terms of the organisation that would soon evolve into the Irish Republican Army. The

reorganisation of the Volunteers had placed a great emphasis on inculcating in its members the sense of being a military force; the organisational requirements of the funeral gave them a chance to put this into practice in public, in a co-ordinated manner and on a large scale. In the days prior to the funeral, Collins could observe that 'Dublin is in the hands of the Volunteers again this week'. For Richard Mulcahy, who fought alongside Ashe during the Rising, who played a major role in organising the funeral and who would later become chief of staff of the Volunteers, the death and funeral of Thomas Ashe 'produced a people effectively organised politically, with a clear political aim and with a Volunteer organisation which was to defend and sustain them'. This was the big picture; for the young Ernie O'Malley, whose Volunteer company had assembled at the top of Whitworth Road alongside the Royal Canal, armed and in full expectation of a confrontation with the British, the more basic reality that 'the Volunteers had held the streets of the capital, had kept order, had marched in the forbidden formations, had worn uniforms' was the most significant lesson to be taken from the day of the funeral. Both were right. Alongside its broader political impact, the funeral of Thomas Ashe gave the re-emerging Irish Volunteers a focal point around which to mobilise in their own right. In that sense, it became another part of the foundation upon which they would continue to build in the years that followed.

John Gibney was formerly Education and Outreach Officer at Glasnevin Cemetery Museum.

Further reading

The Capuchin Annual (1967).

W. Murphy, *Political imprisonment and the Irish, 1912–1921* (Oxford, 2014).

S. Ó Luing, *I die in a good cause: a study of Thomas Ashe, idealist and revolutionary* (Cork, 1970).

The Revolution Papers, 1916–1923: September 1917: The grim death of Thomas Ashe (8 March 2016).

GLASNEVIN CEMETERY'S 'PATRIOT PLOT' AFTER 1916

BY **CONOR DODD**

Some of the best-known graves in Dublin's Glasnevin Cemetery are those within the 'Republican Plot', an area holding the resting places of numerous figures associated with the Irish Republican Brotherhood (IRB), the 1916 Rising, the War of Independence and the Civil War. But what are its origins?

Although Glasnevin's 'Republican Plot' is most often associated with the Easter Rising, it owes its origins not to 1916 but to the aftermath of the Fenian rising of 1867. Following the executions of the 'Manchester Martyrs' at Salford Gaol on 22 November 1867, IRB members purchased an empty grave near the tomb of Daniel O'Connell as the location for a memorial to them. Processions to Glasnevin to commemorate the Manchester Martyrs soon became an impressively large annual event, and in the early 1900s the leading Fenians James Stephens and John O'Leary were buried in the plots alongside the memorial. This particular area of Glasnevin Cemetery had now become a place of importance for separatists, and the enormous funeral in 1915 of the old Fenian Jeremiah O'Donovan Rossa, buried adjacent to Stephens and O'Leary, only served to reinforce the emerging symbolism of this section of the graveyard.

After the Easter Rising, the Irish National Aid Association and Volunteers' Dependants' Fund (INAAVDF) took on the task of caring for the families and for the graves of Volunteers killed during the fighting. In May 1917 they proposed that all those Volunteers killed in the Rising and buried in Glasnevin and elsewhere should be exhumed and buried together in a central plot within the cemetery. Wide-scale exhumations proved impractical, however. The proposal received new impetus in August 1917, when a 'Patriot Graves Association' was formed and made enquiries about purchasing the entire area of graves around what was now being referred to as the 'Patriot Plot' (it would not be dubbed the 'Republican Plot' until the 1920s). The Association committee was a who's who of senior figures in the independence movement, including Count Plunkett, Countess Markievicz, Éamon de Valera, Arthur Griffith, W.T. Cosgrave, Kathleen Clarke, Austin Stack, Margaret Pearse, Áine O'Rahilly, Michael Collins and others. It is probable that these efforts were precipitated by another important burial in the plot, the first since that of Rossa in 1915.

On 9 July 1917 Muriel MacDonagh, the widow of the executed Rising leader Thomas MacDonagh, tragically drowned at Skerries while on a trip organised by the INAAVDF. It seemed natural that she would be buried in Glasnevin. Her funeral on 12 July was attended by many of those who had been released a few weeks previously under the general amnesty of prisoners. Among these and standing in a prominent position at the graveside was Éamon de Valera, who just two days earlier had won the East Clare by-election.

On the same day as the MacDonagh funeral, John Redmond learned of the death of his party colleague and close friend Pat O'Brien MP. Redmond purchased a grave for O'Brien in Glasnevin and the funeral took place two days after that of Mrs MacDonagh. Although it attracted a sizeable attendance it was significantly smaller, and some years later Stephen Gwynn recalled how Redmond

'... came to Dublin for Pat O'Brien's funeral in Glasnevin. Then and then only in his lifetime people saw him publicly break down; he had to be led away from the grave.'

●

Below: A listing of graves of 'those who gave their lives for Ireland', from the Young Ireland rebellion of 1848 to the death of Thomas Ashe, arranged in order to facilitate a visit. Note the cluster of graves in the emerging 'Patriot Plot'. (Glasnevin Trust)

CLÁR NA CUAIRD.

25th NOV

ꞬUIꝹ ꝺꞒ ꞒꞂꞒꞒꞒꞒ ꞒꞂ ꞒꞒꞒꞒꞒ

LIST OF GRAVES in Glasnevin of those
Arranged and number

1.	THE PATRIOT PLOT.		
	James Stephens.	1848-67.	
	John O'Leary.	"	
	O'Donovan Rossa	"	
	The Manchester Martyrs.	1867.	
	The O Rathghaille.	1916.	
	Mrs Thomas MacDonagh.	1917.	
	Thomas Ashe.	1917.	
2.	Anne Devlin		No. of Grave
3.	Terence Bellew MacManus.	1867.	
4.	John O'Mahony.	1867.	
5.	Colour-Sergeant McCarthy.	1867.	
6.	Daniel Reddin.	1867.	
7.	Denis Duggan		
8.	John Keegan Casey ("Leo")	1848.	
9.	Sean Connolly.	1916.	
10.	Patrick Whelan	1916.	CB 103 South
11.	Michael Malone.	1916.	R 40½
12.	James Corcoran.	1916.	G 40½
13.	James Fintan Lalor	1848.	
14.	Chas. Underwood O'Connell	1867.	
15.	John Healy (the boy hero)	1916.	VB 100 Garden section
16.	Stowell Bros. (died from prison treatment)	1867.	84½ & 85
17.	Clarence Mangan		
18.	Frazer (De Jean)		
19.	Stephen Donohoe and his comrades who fell at Tallaght 1867	1867.	CE 197
20.	Edward Duffy	1867.	
21.	Patrick O'Donnell	1882.	JF 56A & 57
22.	Henry Coyle	1916.	DG 45½
23.	Edward Ennis	1916.	AG 24½
24.	Philip Walsh	1916.	FG 24½
25.	John Traynor	1916.	VG 22½

PRICE ONE PENNY. Published by the National Graves' Comm

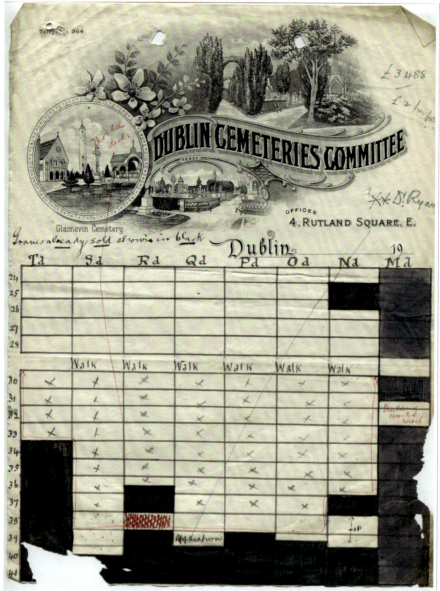

Above: Graves available for purchase in what became Glasnevin Cemetery's 'Republican Plot', c. October 1917. The black boxes indicate graves that have been filled, while 'x' marks the vacant plots available. The grave marked in red on the lower left is that of Thomas Ashe. (Glasnevin Trust)

The political tide was turning, and Redmond's public profile was almost emblematic of the decline and eventual eclipse of the Home Rule movement.

The death of Thomas Ashe in September 1917 resulted in another large-scale funeral to the Patriot Plot. Two days after his death his grave was purchased by John Richard Reynolds, an accountant and member of the IRB who would become an important figure in the development and expansion of the plot. Reynolds's office on College Street was a hub of republican activity before and after 1916, and his responsibilities related, for the most part, to the financial aspects of the revolution. Reynolds had been a member of the 'Wolfe Tone Memorial Committee', the IRB front organisation that had organised the funerals of both O'Donovan Rossa and Ashe.

The efforts to inter those republicans who had died during the 1916 Rising in the plot gradually waned as new 'martyrs' emerged in 1917 and 1918. In January 1918, however, two reinterments did take place—Michael Malone, who had been killed at Mount Street, and James Corcoran, an Irish Citizen Army member killed at St Stephen's Green. It is perhaps apt, given that the burials within the plot reflected the changes under way in post-Rising Ireland, that the final major funeral of this period came in the midst of the 1918 general election. On 9 December Richard Coleman, another veteran of Easter Week, died while interned in Usk Prison in Wales. His death became part of the wider debate around Sinn Féin's general election campaign. This culminated on 15 December, the day after the election, in Coleman's interment in the Patriot Plot with a huge crowd in attendance. The exact impact of Coleman's death on the election is indeterminable, but its prominence in the week prior to voting was not insignificant.

In the years that followed, the Patriot Plot would continue to mirror the wider political turmoil of the revolution and its aftermath. The original wish to have all of those rebels who died during the Rising buried alongside one another within the plot was not realised, but its development throughout 1917 and 1918 secured its position as a place of significance and importance for those who would take part in the War of Independence and the Civil War. The development, ownership and inheritance of the legitimacy of what came to be known as the 'Republican Plot' would become even more complicated during the years that followed.

Conor Dodd is Resident Historian at Glasnevin Cemetery Museum.

Further reading

L.M. Griffith & C. Wallace (eds), *Grave matters: death and dying in Dublin, 1500 to the present* (Dublin, 2016).

S. Mac Thomáis, *Glasnevin: Ireland's necropolis* (Dublin, 2010).

B. Ní Rathaille, 'A complicated patch of land: the evolution of the republican plot in Glasnevin Cemetery 1916–1930', *Dublin Historical Record* **69** (2) (2016), 236–48.

IRELAND AND WWI

'What little enthusiasm had ever existed for the war had evaporated by 1916, but the cumulative impact of reservists recalled to the colours and recruitment in 1914 and 1915 meant that by 1917 payments to soldiers' dependants, including an increasing number of widows, was the second largest source of income in Dublin's tenements after labourers' wages.'

Image: Recruitment posters on a wall by the Four Courts.

Working and living conditions in Dublin 1916–18.

THE WAGES OF WAR

BY **PADRAIG YEATES**

One unexpected bonus of the Easter Rising in Dublin was that it ended a protracted building strike. With 3,000 workers involved, it was by far the largest industrial dispute of the year. Unions were seeking pay rises of between 2d and 1d an hour, and the employers had offered between a farthing and a ha'penny. After the devastation wrought by the Rising there was an urgent need to rebuild the city, and the British government used the Munitions Act to impose a settlement. The arbitrator, Captain Fairbairn Downie, awarded an increase of a penny ha'penny an hour, much nearer the workers' demands than the employers' offer, but a penny of it was a 'war bonus' that would end with hostilities. It still represented an increase of almost 15%, bringing the average earnings of building workers to £115 17s 0d a year.

The move was partly an effort to address civil unrest in the city, but also to ensure the completion of the National Shell Factory at Park Gate. After the Rising some senior officials in Dublin Castle queried the wisdom of such a move, but the minister for munitions, David Lloyd George, brushed their objections aside, telling them that he needed shells for the front and that workers earning war bonuses would be too busy making money to make revolution. He was proven wrong on the last count, but it is true to say that, if Dublin was a late beneficiary of the British war economy, it benefited nevertheless and, paradoxically, because the city was not essential to the war effort it had the best of two worlds. The 1915 Munitions Act granted enormous powers to the British government and the labour movement had agreed to suspend the strike tactic in strategically sensitive industries for the duration of the war in return for union recognition, while employers abandoned the lockout tactic and accepted binding arbitration to resolve disputes. Dublin benefited from the labour shortages, although there was never full employment as there was in Belfast and Britain. On the other hand, the government never felt it needed to use the draconian measures occasionally resorted to in Britain, such as imprisonment or conscription of militant shop stewards in crucial industrial sectors.

The case of the new National Shell Factory at Park Gate is a good example. It produced half a million shells by 1919, or 80% of Irish output, but British plants produced 16.5 million in the second half of 1915 alone, when they were far from reaching full capacity. Yet munitions work did provide exceptional employment opportunities for well over 1,000 women at the Dublin plant, and for another 300 in a smaller, privately owned plant run by the Dublin Dockyard Company. These women could earn up to £3 a week on piecework, over £1 a week more than the average building worker and more than many skilled men, let alone casual labourers on 15s or 20s.

Some of these 'munitioneers' were no doubt among the young working-class women 'going astray' and enjoying themselves in the 'low saloons' of O'Connell Street. They evoked a response from middle-class lady patrollers alarmed at the war's impact on public morality. These women usually comprised strong supporters of female suffrage but otherwise ranged from evangelical Protestants to republican militants, anxious to protect vulnerable working-class women but also to keep them in their place.

Unlike Britain, where 'munitioneers' were drawn from all social classes except the very well-off, middle-class women in Dublin did not seek factory work, except in a voluntary capacity on welfare and canteen committees, to look after their less fortunate working-class sisters. These volunteers were later replaced by full-time, paid welfare superintendents such as Margaret Culhane, a sister of Hanna Sheehy Skeffington. When questions were asked in the House of Commons about her suitability, Lloyd George's parliamentary secretary, Worthington Evans, assured MPs that all the proper procedures had been observed and added that she had made significant improvements on her voluntary predecessors.

Among these improvements was a switch from twelve-hour to eight-hour shifts to maintain 24-hour production. It had been found that the productivity of women working twelve hours was often poorer than those working eight, as well as leading to increased illness and absenteeism. Little was done to protect them from the toxic chemicals that bleached their hair and, more importantly, corroded their lungs—but then the same could be said about many male occupations of the period.

While union organisation and militancy grew rapidly in such a favourable climate, radical political activism could act as a brake. For instance, while female membership of unions rose from just under 5,000 in 1914 to 17,000 by 1917, the Irish Women Workers Union (IWWU) almost disappeared because its key activists were in the Citizen Army. Once Helena Molony was released from prison IWWU membership rose to over 2,000 in 1917, and to over 5,000 when Louie Bennett took over and focused on industrial organisation.

Other unions grew significantly after 1916, although the spectacular growth of the ITGWU was mainly outside Dublin, thanks, once more, to a British government initiative aimed at maintaining industrial peace and safeguarding food supplies, in this case with the establishment of agricultural wages boards. Dublin suf-

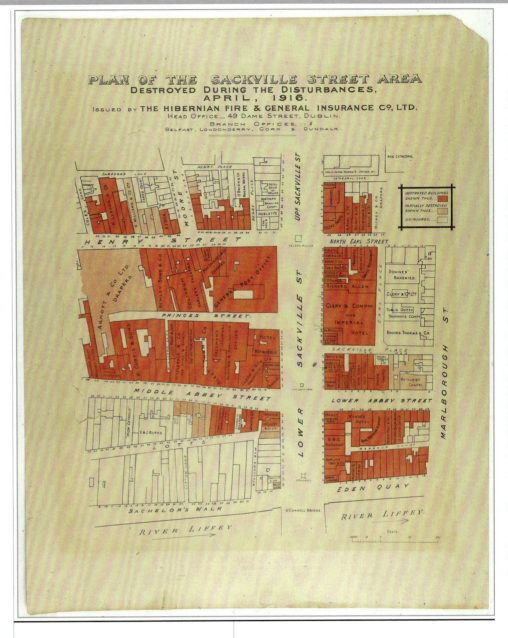

fered the worst of both worlds where food supplies were concerned, failing to benefit from the agricultural boom of the war years but suffering from the consequences of higher prices.

British wholesalers could use economies of scale to pay Irish farmers higher prices and still charge consumers less, so that Irish eggs and meat were cheaper in London or Liverpool than in Dublin. Not that many Dubliners could afford such luxuries. By 1917 black bread, or 'war bread', had become part of the staple diet, while potatoes were a luxury food. Although the government introduced price controls in late 1916

it did little to enforce them, as it had no interest in antagonising Irish farmers and fuelling unrest in rural Ireland. Unfortunately for Dubliners, Ireland lacked the large urban constituencies that ensured consumer interests some protection in Britain. During the winter of 1917, for instance, the official price of potatoes was £9 a ton but they sold for

● Above: Map of Dublin city centre, showing the buildings destroyed by fire during the Rising. (Dublin City Library and Archives)

● Opposite page: The new National Shell Factory at Park Gate. (Imperial War Museum)

Top: Munitions workers football team from Waterford, pictured in 1917. (NLI)

Above: Female munitions workers at the National Shell Factory in Dublin take a break outdoors during the First World War. (Imperial War Museum)

to be suspended until a new rate was struck. This affected 10,000 children and caused increased malnutrition among families dependent on dry black bread and even blacker tea. The ITGWU reopened its food kitchen in Liberty Hall and private charities, British as well as Irish, struggled to fill the gap.

Coal now cost as much as the weekly rent in many homes and the Corporation closed its public baths in Tara Street, denying locals not only the chance of a bath but somewhere to wash their clothes. Hospitals reduced ambient temperatures on the wards, and even businesses dependent on electricity and gas were forced to close early.

But the most crucial battle of all was over milk. It was the cheapest form of protein available in the city and vitally important for children. While overall mortality rates in the city fell during the war, at least until the influenza pandemic struck in 1918, infant mortality rates rose. Nor was Dublin alone. As Lord Rhondda, the minister for food, admitted in 1916, more babies were dying of disease, malnutrition and neglect than men at the front. There should have been no shortages in Dublin, with over 200 dairies and 7,500 head of cattle, plus ready access to surrounding farms, but the Cow Keepers' and Dairymen's Association was the most hated organisation in the city, with members regularly prosecuted for overcharging and adulterating milk. Pressure on fodder supplies saw the official price of milk rise from 3d a quart to 4d in late 1916. A government Milk Prices Order only aggravated the situation, as the dairymen started selling their milch cows in England.

It was only when P.T. Daly, head of the ITGWU insurance section and a Labour councillor, was released from internment at the end of 1916 that things improved. As chairman of the city's Food Committee, he instructed inspectors to prosecute dairy owners under the Food, Drugs and Margarine Act rather than the city bylaws. Convictions under the Act incurred prison sentences rather than fines. The first prison sentences

£13–£14 in the shops. Eventually the British army released some of its stocks onto the Dublin market to force prices down.

Imports of items such as coal, tea and tobacco were affected by the German U-boat campaign and the consequent prohibitive costs of shipping. Restrictive practices in Dublin's distributive trade added another 25% to the total cost for carrying supplies the mile or so from the ships to the shops.

By 1917 the cost of compensation to property owners for the destruction wrought by the Rising was seriously undermining Dublin Corporation's ability to provide relief to its worst-off citizens. In early 1917 school meals in tenement areas had

for dairy owners in ten years were handed down and, after three such convictions, the abuses ceased. Nevertheless, prices continued to rise, peaking at 8d a quart in the winter of 1917, compared with 3d a year earlier. Even the Irish Parliamentary Party and *Irish Times* now called for controls. The government duly banned milk exports and imposed maximum prices of 4d and 5d a quart, depending on milk quality. A further increase of 1d was sanctioned in October 1918.

P.T. Daly was also involved in the battle against immorality, or at least its health-related consequences. As chair of the Corporation's Public Health Committee, he funded two new wards at Dr Steevens' Hospital to treat sexually transmitted diseases. These supplemented existing facilities such as the Westmoreland Lock Hospital, which catered mainly for prostitutes and their children. The new clinics did not open until 1919 but within a year attendances by men had risen fivefold and by women tenfold. Nationalist propagandists blamed the licentious British soldiery but infection rates peaked in 1934.

Housing was an even bigger problem. The financial cost of the war, and the Rising, meant that only 327 Corporation dwellings were built, mainly after 1916. Most of them were modest one- and two-bedroom affairs, while nearly 1,000 tenements were closed as unsafe, leaving 3,563 families homeless.

What little enthusiasm had ever existed for the war had evaporated by 1916, but the cumulative impact of reservists recalled to the colours and recruitment in 1914 and 1915 meant that by 1917 payments to soldiers' dependants, including an increasing number of widows, was the second largest source of income in Dublin's tenements after labourers' wages. War Office inspectors, often tipped off by hostile neighbours, would regularly raid homes to catch unfaithful wives and widows. Anyone caught lost their separation payments.

This reflected a broader cultural consensus across the political and social divide, with many Dubliners resentful of the corrosive effects of the war on public morality. By October 1916 Catholic and Protestant church bodies were united in demanding more rigorous censorship of theatres and cinemas, leading a badly cash-strapped Corporation to appoint censors, supplemented by Dublin Vigilance Committee volunteers. Theoretically managers could lose their licences but, as many of these entertainments were funded by the War Office for the troops, the shows went ahead, feeding growing resentment at what the 1916 martyr James Connolly had described as 'the corruption of the oppressor'.

One final scourge that wrought more deaths in the city than the war or the Rising was the Spanish 'flu pandemic. While the mortality rates had fallen fairly steadily from the first winter of the war, when they stood at 31.4 per thousand, to 20.4 by the summer of 1918, they shot up again to 32.7 in July and peaked in the winter of 1918/19 at 37.7, when more people died in the city than were born.

Padraig Yeates is the author of A city in civil war: Dublin 1921–4 *(Gill & Macmillan, 2015).*

Further reading

D. Fitzpatrick, 'Irish consequences of the Great War', *Irish Historical Studies* **156** (November 2015).
A. Gregory & S. Paseta, *Ireland and the Great War* (Manchester, 2002).
J. Horne (ed.), *Our war* (Dublin, 2008).
P. Yeates, *A city in wartime: Dublin 1914–1918* (Dublin, 2011).

●

Below: The Portrait Gallery at Dublin Castle became a Red Cross hospital during the First World War. (Imperial War Museum)

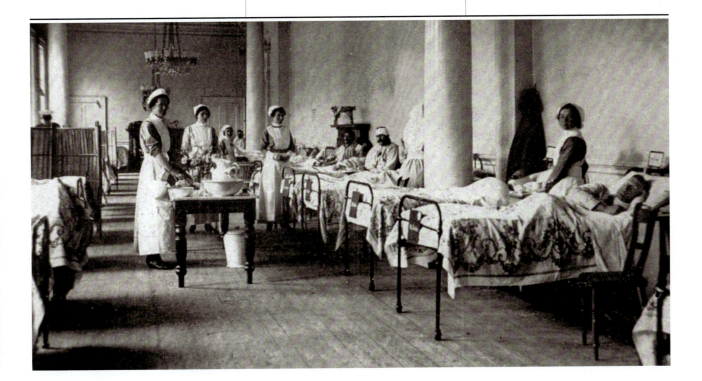

A fierce naval struggle took place off Ireland throughout 1917 that was to determine the outcome of the war.

THE WAR AT SEA

BY **MICHAEL KENNEDY**

In February 1917 Germany began a campaign of unrestricted submarine warfare to enhance its ongoing naval blockade of the British Isles. Germany's U-boats attempted to cut Britain's maritime lifelines and force her to surrender. Vessels were attacked without warning and shipping was sunk by U-boats without distinction of nationality. By summer 1917, Allied shipping losses had increased so rapidly that it seemed that Germany might force Britain to sue for peace.

Responding to the German submarine onslaught, Britain's naval chiefs began marshalling merchant shipping into convoys. This helped to reduce sinkings, as did better intelligence and, after April 1917, the deployment of United States destroyers to the western approaches to assist the Royal Navy. Combined with the growing exhaustion of the U-boat fleet, these developments meant that by late 1917 the Allies had the upper hand in the war at sea. This was not evident at the time, however. Only in retrospect could Lloyd George write in his war memoirs that the great Allied triumph of 1917 was the gradual beating off of the U-boat.

Ireland's lighthouse service, the Commissioners of Irish Lights, today known as Irish Lights, was in 1917, as today, responsible for the provision of aids to navigation and maritime safety around the island of Ireland. Through the First World War its lighthouse-keepers and lightshipmen were on the front line of the war at sea. As the U-boat campaign increased its momentum during

1917, they witnessed an unforgiving naval battle around Ireland. Facing dangers from U-boats and mines, retrieving corpses and flotsam, and helping shipwrecked sailors to safety, light-keepers and lightshipmen saw at first hand the human and physical cost of war. Their reports, held in the archives of Irish Lights, give a unique local and international perspective on the war at sea off Ireland.

Irish Lights staff faced real dangers from the intensifying naval conflict. On 2 March 1917, J.J. Duff, master of the Coningbeg lightship, on station off the Saltee Islands, reported that a mine had exploded beneath his vessel, lifting it out of the water. Duff and his crew were unharmed, but the Commissioners knew the trying circumstances in which they operated. Captain Deane, the Inspector of Lights, wrote that Duff reported the explosion as a common occurrence. He was correct. The Coningbeg sent regular reports of submarines, mines, naval encounters and the rescue of shipwrecked seafarers to Irish Lights headquarters in Dublin.

As shipping bound for Britain had to route through the western and north-western approaches, U-boats could lie in wait off Ireland's coast. Throughout 1917, U-boats hunted shipping in the Irish Sea south to the Tuskar Rock, then west to the Fastnet and on to Loop Head. They also operated in the north-western approaches off Tory Island, off Belfast Lough and south towards Dundrum Bay.

The strategic value of the resources that Britain was losing through submarine sinkings can be extrapolated from even one instance. On 29 March 1917 the *Lincolnshire*, bound from New York to Le Havre,

● Right: A coloured postcard that juxtaposes the destroyer flotilla in Bantry Bay during the First World War with the tranquil domesticity of the Irish thatched cottage. (Fergus O'Connor/Adrian Healy)

● Left: Hook Head Lighthouse in the early twentieth century; it was unable to assist as a Royal Navy trawler, the *George Melvin*, struck a mine and sank in less than a minute. (NLI)

was sunk by *U-57* off Dunmore East. Her crew were saved, but her cargo—3,000 tons of copper, 1,000 tons each of cartridges, lead and gun cotton, as well as an amount of machinery—was lost. It shows what one successful U-boat attack could achieve in reducing Allied access to resources.

Light-keepers often saw small episodes which caught the sudden horror of war. On a summer's evening in July 1917, Hook Head and Dunmore East lighthouses watched, unable to assist, as a Royal Navy trawler, the *George Melvin*, struck a mine and sank in less than a minute. A sole survivor was rescued.

An American destroyer commander operating out of Queenstown (Cobh) wrote in summer 1917 that his patrol zone off the Fastnet contained wreckage, several boats adrift and oily streaks. It was not a unique report. In early November on the east coast at Rockabill, off Skerries, Co. Dublin, Principal Keeper King heard two explosions, though he could not see a ship in distress. Two hours later he sighted wreckage, including life-rafts, hatches and timber.

Captain Coventry of the Irish Lights tender *Alexandra* asked a senior Irish Lights official to impress on the Commissioners that conditions along the Irish coast were now very different from 1916. Arriving in Queenstown, Coventry saw mine-

sweepers at work. They exploded a mine close to *Alexandra* when she was moored off Daunt Rock at the entrance to Cork Harbour. It was one of ten mines they detonated that day.

Throughout 1917 U-boats regularly mined the entrances to Waterford and Cork harbours. The results were devastating. On 18 February 1917 the naval trawler *Clifton* hit a mine close to the Daunt Rock lightship. There was a solitary survivor. The Daunt's master reported that they picked up one body; the remainder of the crew were lost.

While proceeding to the Skellig Rocks on 10 March 1917, the Irish Lights tender *Ierne* picked up fourteen men from the Norwegian coal-carrier *Storstad*. In a waterlogged lifeboat, they had been adrift for two days in heavy seas after being sunk 83km south-west of the Fastnet by *U-62*, commanded by Kapitanleutnant Ernst Hashagen. Hashagen refused any help to the men, even to tow their lifeboat towards safety, and left them to their fate. They were exhausted and suffering from exposure. *Ierne*'s crew gave the stranded sailors food and first aid and landed them at Valentia. *Storstad* was the first of 45 ships sunk by *U-62* in 1917 alone, one statistic showing the massive impact the U-boat had on Allied shipping.

The most troubling episode for

Berehaven Bantry Bay.

Irish Lights during the First World War occurred on 28 March 1917, when the South Arklow lightship *Guillemot* was sunk by *UC-65*. Having observed the lightship warning passing shipping of its activity in the area, and having sunk ten ships nearby that day, the U-boat pulled alongside the lightship and ordered the crew to leave. After a search for secret documents, two bombs were placed in *Guillemot*. They did not sink her. *UC-65* finished *Guillemot*

● Above: Fleet of British Navy ships off Berehaven, Co. Cork. (NLI)

● Opposite page: American sailors on shore leave in Berehaven in the winter of 1917. They have beer and female company, but it doesn't quite match Havana or Manila! (Ralph Gifford)

off with five shots into her bow.

James Rossiter, master of the South Arklow lightship, reported that his duty as a British sailor was plain; he was desirous of doing his bit for the Empire. His action in warning shipping about the presence of U-boats doubtless saved lives. He was warmly commended for his action by the Commissioners of Irish Lights. After the sinking, Irish Lights cryptically announced that the South Arklow lightship had 'disappeared'— but not for eternity. Rediscovered during the Infomar survey of the Irish Sea, *Guillemot* now lies almost intact, upright, facing north–south, in 51.5m of water.

The U-boat campaign reached its zenith in April 1917. German submarines now acted with impunity off Ireland. On 27 April the Mizen

Head Fog Signal Station reported a German submarine shelling the cargo ship *Quantock* in full view of the station for two hours. A second vessel was attacked by the U-boat but escaped towards Berehaven after returning fire.

Further up the coast, at Tory Island off Donegal, two lifeboats from *Sebek*, torpedoed without warning by *U-70*, and the Norwegian barque *Acadia*, sunk by gunfire by *U-52*, made landfall on 23 and 24 April. A day earlier, survivors from the Norwegian *Vestelv* put ashore. Her captain described how they had been boarded by the commander of *U-93* twenty miles north-west of Tory. He ordered them to take to their boats, placed bombs amidships and blew *Vestelv* up. The commander had to stop his men from looting the ship before sinking her.

U-boats attacked as and when they desired with devastating effect off Ireland through the summer of 1917. On 3 May the mate of the Skulmartin lightship off County Down saw a submarine four miles to the south sink three steamships, one at 4.25am, one at 4.35am and one at 5.30am; the U-boat also engaged a passing naval patrol vessel.

The Royal Navy began to marshal shipping into convoys from May 1917. There was a sharp drop in tonnage sunk that month, but this was most likely because U-boats could not sustain the tremendous effort of their sinkings during April. It took time for the convoys to become effective. U-boats still had an effective hunting ground off the Irish coast. Shipping losses in June 1917 (687,507 gross registered tons) were the second highest for the whole of the war. Torpedoing and surface attacks on shipping continued unabated around the Irish coast. Submarine sightings and reports of minelaying by U-boats were continually received by Irish Lights.

Waterford Harbour was a popular location for German minelaying. In July 1917 *UC-42* mined the mouth of the harbour. After a sham minesweeping operation, signals were sent that the mines had been removed. The ruse worked. Late on 4 August 1917 the Dunmore East lighthouse observed a remarkable event. German minelaying submarine *UC-44*, commanded by Kapitanleutnant Tebbenjohannes, returned to replace the supposedly removed mines. Surfacing to plot his course, he detonated one of his own recently laid mines, fatally damaging his own U-boat.

Tebbenjohannes was picked up; his crew drowned. A salvage operation brought *UC-44* to the surface and she was beached at Dunmore East. The Admiralty picked up considerable technical and operational intelligence from *UC-44*, including its logbooks. These showed how easily U-boats could operate around Britain and Ireland and evade detection. On 29 August Hook Tower saw at first hand just how suddenly a

U-boat could strike. At 2pm a large four-masted barque under naval escort was torpedoed five miles to the south. The sailing ship disappeared immediately.

Where a ship's crew were saved, the personal impact on Irish Lights staff was considerable. On 25 September the shipwrecked crew of three from the schooner *Mary Grace* boarded the Coningbeg lightship. They had been sunk by a submarine the previous evening. From March to November 1917 Coningbeg took on board 60 shipwrecked sailors from five ships, providing them with clothes and tobacco and food from their own rations. In total they provided 58lbs of bread, 40lbs of corned beef, 4 stone of sugar, 8lbs of tea and 13lbs of butter.

It was often a pitiful tale when reporting shipwrecked sailors. When the 28 surviving crew of the *Carlo* boarded the Coningbeg lightship on 13 November 1917, its master reported that half of them were naked. He and the crew gave all the clothing they had to them, adding: 'You would pity the poor men if you had seen them shivering in the boat with the cold for want of clothing'.

The final months of 1917 seemed to bring an improvement for the Allies in the war at sea. The protective function of convoys was now established and effective. Yet it was by no means clear as 1917 drew to a close that the U-boat campaign had

reached its zenith and that the victory of the Allies in the war at sea was more likely.

The experience of the war at sea around Ireland during 1917 shows how the grand narrative of the naval conflict and the less well-known local narratives can combine through the prism by which Ireland's light-keepers and lightship men witnessed the war at sea around their coast. In the ongoing decade of commemoration and reflection, this year we should remember the ferocity of the battle they saw off our coasts 100 years ago. Their experience of 1917 around Ireland shows how very real and dangerous that battle was. It also places the First World War right on Ireland's coastline and shores and brings that conflict back into our historical consciousness in a vivid and often horrifying manner.

Michael Kennedy is the Executive Editor of the Royal Irish Academy's Documents on Irish Foreign Policy series.

Further reading

M. Kennedy & E. Kinsella, *Safety at sea through war and upheaval: Irish Lights 1911–1923* (Dún Laoghaire, 2016).

R. Stokes, *U-Boat Alley: the U-boat war in the Irish Channel during World War 1* (Gorey, 2004).

J. Terraine, *Business in great waters* (London, 1989).

www.u-boat.net

Irish Labour and the October Revolution.

BOLSHEVISM AS FOREIGN POLICY

BY **EMMET O'CONNOR**

Support for the Bolsheviks was Labour's first foreign policy. This was due primarily to the Socialist Party of Ireland (SPI), a ginger group within the Irish Trades Union Congress and Labour Party (ITUCLP). The SPI was the third of the name. The first had been founded in 1904 after the departure of James Connolly to America and the implosion of his Irish Socialist Republican Party. The second was launched in 1909, and associated with Connolly on his return from America in 1910.

In January 1917 the party was revived, and William O'Brien was elected chairman. Almost certainly it was integral to O'Brien's plan to cloak himself in the mantle of Labour's national martyr as he rebuilt the Irish Transport and General Workers' Union (ITGWU) after the dislocation of Easter Week. As union membership expanded and Europe moved left, the SPI evolved as a vanguard, attracting many of the ITGWU's rising stars. Peadar O'Donnell recalled: 'I did not like

him [O'Brien] but I respected him. We regarded him as the Lenin of the Labour movement. The Petrograd revolution had occurred: we admired it and looked to someone like O'Brien to lead the way.' Initially, the SPI drew its ideas from Connolly's syndicalism, but after November 1917 it showed a livelier interest in Soviet Russia. Cathal O'Shannon, party ideologist and editor of the ITGWU's *Voice of Labour* and the *Watchword of Labour*, insisted on its Bolshevism. As the best-connected Marxist party in Irish history, the SPI was well placed to radicalise the Labour leadership, and that leadership was searching for political relevance.

Formed in 1912–14 when the Irish Trades Union Congress simply added 'and Labour Party' to its name, the ITUCLP had no electoral machinery and was anxious to find its ideological feet in an obviously propitious time. The world war was creating a manpower shortage and, after years of hardship, wages were catching up with price inflation as the government released more money into the economy to keep the war effort going. There was, too, a heightening of political consciousness against a backdrop of revolution at home and abroad, and a feeling that the end of the war would usher in a new age of the people throughout Europe. Tom Johnson, SPI member and the ITUCLP's *de facto* secretary, was eager for Labour to reflect the prevailing climate.

By early 1917 various efforts were under way to re-establish the international socialist unity that had collapsed in August 1914. For Irish Labour, it was an opportunity to assert its radicalism and its nationalism. In February the Dublin trades council called for Irish self-determination and separate Irish representation at all 'International Labour' conferences. Following the February revolution in Russia, the ITUCLP sent its congratulations to the recently established Petrograd Soviet, and when the Soviet and a Dutch–Scandinavian socialist committee called for an international labour conference to meet in Stockholm, the ITUCLP executive agreed to send

a delegation, mandated to 'seek to establish the Irish Labour Party as a distinct unit in the international labour movement' and to support 'the Russian Conference of Workers' and Soldiers' Delegates' war policy of peace without annexations or indemnities, on the basis of national self-determination. When the decision was endorsed after heated debate at the ITUCLP annual conference in Derry in August, it was clear that positions on Russia hinged on attitudes towards Germany, the world war and the national question. Vigorous opposition came from Redmondites and Ulster unionists, while the great majority of delegates were less impressed by the overthrow of the tsar than by the anti-war stance of the Bolsheviks. In the event, the Irish delegates were denied passports by the British government, but O'Brien attended the Leeds conference convened by the British United Socialist Party to salute the February revolution, and insisted on recognition as an Irish representative and on calling for the release of Irish political prisoners.

Enthusiasm for Russia only grew with the October Revolution. It helped that the Vatican regarded the disestablishment of the Russian Orthodox Church as an opportunity, and sought a concordat with the Soviet government permitting Roman clergy to proselytise in Russia. Not until Josef Stalin denounced religion in 1929—as part of the mobilisation for the five-year plan—did Pope Pius XI and the Irish clergy unleash a concerted assault on communism. In its first editorial response on 15 December 1917, the *Voice of Labour* encapsulated the popular outlook, up to 1920 at least, in treating the Bolsheviks as synonymous with 'Labour'. Tsarism, of course, had been

● Above right: Commemorations of the 1917 October Revolution in Russia were held in Dublin. (NLI).

● Opposite page: Illustration from the cover of *Bezbozhnik u stanka*, a 1920s–1930s Soviet atheist magazine: 'Long live the World October Revolution'. (New York Public Library)

a byword for oppression, social and national, and from an Irish republican perspective there was not much difference between the tsar and the successor governments of Georgy Lvov and Alexander Kerensky. By contrast, the Bolsheviks, with their opposition to the world war and support for national self-determination, seemed to chime with Sinn Féin.

Labour made its first contact with the Bolsheviks in January 1918, when a joint ITUCLP–SPI deputation met Maxim Litvinov, the Soviet plenipotentiary in London, and appealed for Russian backing for their objectives at international conferences. Litvinov had taught languages for three years in the Jewish Jaffe Public Elementary School in Belfast and delighted the Irish with his admiration for Connolly. Already one could detect differences of policy between Narkomindel, the Soviet foreign ministry, and the commu-

MS 11,323/4/1

THE SOCIALIST PARTY OF IRELAND

(cumannact na h-éireann).

OBJECT:
To replace the present chaotic state of society by an organised Commonwealth in Ireland, in which the Land, Railways and all other instruments of production, distribution and exchange shall be owned and controlled by the whole people.

PRIVATE AND CONFIDENTIAL

It is, indeed, certain that industrial society will not permanently survive without a systematic organisation. The mere conflict of private interests will never produce a well-ordered Commonwealth of Labour.
—*J. Kells Ingram.*

At the epoch making meeting in the Mansion House, Dublin, on the 19th April, a labour delegate will propose the following resolutions :

I.   That this meeting, consisting of the true representatives of the Irish people, endorse the principle for which James Connolly lived and died, namely, the principle of the abolition of Capitalism in this country :—

" One of these slave birth-marks is a belief in the capitalist system of society ; the Irishman frees himself from such a mark when he realises the truth that a capitalist system is the most foreign they have in Ireland." (Labour in Irish History," by James Connolly, page 10.)

II.   That accordingly each person present pledges himself to divest himself of his land or other property and to hold same on trust for all free Irishmen and Irishwomen.

III.   That in order to further the above objects, and to show the priests of Ireland what is their true work for faith and fatherland, the permission of James Larkin be obtained to the publication of the following articles from the " Irish Worker " of 13th December, 1913 :—

" Do not forget that to-day the Church is as commercial in its organization as any limited liability company in this city. Tell the clergy to come down off that

---

nists. Soviet diplomats were happy to deal with Dáil Éireann and the ITUCLP, whereas the Bolsheviks were supposed to be plotting their downfall. The contradiction would become ever more apparent after V.I. Lenin launched the Third International, later the Communist International or Comintern, in 1919. For the moment, Labour could be as ambiguous as the Soviets. On 4 February 1918 the SPI convened a rally in Dublin's Mansion House to welcome the Bolshevik revolution.

The attendance of some 10,000 'far exceeded the too modest expectations of the promoters', and the crowd spilled out onto Dawson Street, lingering late into the night to savour the atmosphere. As Johnson put it: '[It] set the pace for and determined the international policy of the Labour movement in Ireland'. Johnson himself added liberally to the giddiness in a way that belied his role as the very moderate ideologist of the ITUCLP in the decade after Easter Week. On 23

February, the *Voice of Labour* featured his article 'If the Bolsheviks came to Ireland'. 'We acclaim the Russian revolution,' he gushed, 'and our hearts respond to the call of the Russian people to join with the workers throughout war stricken Europe in dethroning Imperialism *and* Capitalism in our respective countries.'

A proactive foreign policy took shape in late 1918. Two hundred and forty delegates attended the ITUCLP's annual conference in Waterford in August, compared with 99 the previous year. O'Brien's presidential address strained to do justice to the sense of history, invoking Connolly and his influence on 'the great Russian revolution'. The conference called for the re-establishment of the Second International and an ITUCLP–SPI committee was created as the 'Irish section of the International'. Having a presence in the revived International became extremely important to Labour over the next six months. Arguably the reluctance to grasp the nettle of domestic politics intensified the desire to be seen as dynamic on the international stage. With a psychological aversion to confrontation, Johnson was adept at combining rhetorical radicalism with tactical procrastination, and was the key man behind the ITUCLP executive's decision to recommend withdrawal from the 1918 general election.

The special conference which pulled Labour out of the election also endorsed a lengthy 'statement of international aims', calling for peace on 'the Russian formula' of national self-determination and no annexations or indemnities, protesting at the 'capitalist outlawry' of Soviet Russia, and urging the International Socialist Bureau, the permanent organisation of the Second International, which had survived the implosion of August 1914, to 'call the International together without further delay'. It also changed the name of the ITUCLP to the Irish Labour Party and Trade Union Congress. Playing the international card was an easy, non-contentious way of asserting Labour's political identity. Conversely, all of the speakers opposing withdrawal made the point that without MPs Labour's voice in a revived International would be diminished. Some argued that this would weaken Ireland's case for self-determination, and there was clearly a feeling that Labour could make a unique contribution in advancing the national cause through the International. Johnson conceded: 'The position of labour at the International was undoubtedly a very serious one. Undoubtedly it almost overbalanced all the other questions and all the other arguments against taking part in the elections.'

Once the armistice was signed on 11 November, Johnson was despatched to London to meet Camille Huysmans, secretary of the International Socialist Bureau. Huysmans told Johnson to 'prepare our case and send our delegation to the Congress', which would meet in the Volkshaus in Berne, Switzerland, in February 1919. On 23 December 1918, the SPI's executive nominated O'Brien and O'Shannon to a 'Hands off Russia' conference in London on 18 January, and J.J. Hughes as its delegate to Berne. On 28 December the ITUCLP executive appointed Thomas MacPartlin, O'Brien, O'Shannon and Johnson to Berne. The last three were also given credentials as SPI comrades.

Berne was Labour's greatest foreign policy triumph. To strengthen the Irish voice in the Volkshaus, Dáil Éireann adopted the Democratic Programme as its social manifesto. Sinn Féin believed that the Paris Peace Talks would listen to the International, if only to keep workers out of Bolshevism, and the socialists might help the Dáil's envoy gain admittance to the talks. The Irish at Berne canvassed for recognition for the republic, and lobbied the British Labour Party to replace Home Rule with self-determination as its position on Ireland. On the main issue at Berne, the Irish sided with the left minority, voting against a motion for parliamentary democracy as it 'tended to condemn the Soviet system of government', and signing the Adler/Longuet resolution

demanding a 'dictatorship of the proletariat'. Proud of its good work, the Labour Party and Congress published the pamphlet *Irish Labour in its international relations: in the era of the Second International and the Bolshevik Revolution* in 1919. The collection of policy documents and reports illustrated the interconnection of the national question and foreign policy.

Johnson's ardour for the Bolshevik theme cooled after Berne. The word 'soviet', meaning 'council' in Russian, was popularised in Ireland by the Petrograd Soviet, and by 1919 it was being applied to a variety of actions and situations, including workplace occupations or trades councils which assumed a territorial administration, such as during the Limerick general strike of 1919. Critically, it was synonymous with direct action that threatened the authority of union officialdom, or what the communists themselves would later term 'rank and file tendencies'. On the political side, too, the situation turned complicated. To pre-empt a revival of the Second International, Lenin hurriedly convened the Third International in March 1919. One of the 39 groups invited was described as 'the revolutionary elements in the Irish workers' organizations'. Lenin was determined that this International would not be another talking shop but the general staff of the global revolution, and, in time, a world party. The Executive Committee of the Communist International clarified what it meant to be a communist, stipulated that affiliates could have no truck with the social democrats and held out the prospect of generous financial sponsorship. In May 1919 the SPI split, and the breakaway Revolutionary SPI became one of several fringe-left factions that competed for Moscow's favour. At its annual conference in 1920, the Labour Party and Trade Union Congress executive cited division as its reason for not affiliating to either the Second or Third International. A motion challenging its specious neutrality was rejected by 97–54 votes.

For the Labour Party, it was the

beginning of over 40 years of isolation from the international socialist movement. The series of lost strikes in the slump of 1921–3 gutted Labour's radicalism. During the 1930s, international links were associated with socialism and deemed inherently suspicious. The years of Bolshevism as foreign policy were recalled only to embarrass the leadership.

Emmet O'Connor is Senior Lecturer at the School of English, History and Politics at the University of Ulster, Magee College.

Further reading

Cork Workers' Club, *Irish Labour in its international relations: in the era of the Second International and the Bolshevik Revolution* (Cork, 1919).

E. O'Connor, *Reds and the Green: Ireland, Russia, and the Communist Internationals, 1919–43* (Dublin, 2004).

●
Above: Tom Johnson was leader of the Socialist Party of Ireland. (NLI)

●
Opposite page: Socialist Party of Ireland circular, 1917. (NLI)

THE CAMPAIGN AGAINST CONSCRIPTION 1918

BY **MARY McAULIFFE**

'Thoroughly roused by bitter animosity and resolution'.

In early 1918, despite the continuing unrest, there were demands in the House of Commons, from British public opinion and in the British media that conscription be extended to Ireland. Senior military and police leaders who were aware of the Irish situation warned that conscription would be 'bitterly opposed by the united Nationalists and Clergy', but, as Charles Townsend writes, at 'no point did the cabinet seem to worry about the advisability of training a vast number of potential dissidents'. Indeed, Field Marshal Lord French, commander-in-chief of the Home Forces, was determined to implement conscription despite recognising that 'the country would be thoroughly roused by bitter animosity and resolution'. Sir Henry Wilson, chief of staff of the Armed Forces, badly needed 100,000–150,000 reinforcements on the Western Front, and declared himself not afraid to take hundreds of thousands of 'recalcitrant conscripted Irishmen' into his army of 2.5 million. Although the Irish political leaders, the church and the media bluntly said that introducing conscription into Ireland was 'an act of insanity' (*London Times*, 8 April 1918), the Military Service Bill was passed by the House of Commons on 15 April 1918. The implementation of conscription in Ireland was now a very immediate reality.

The Ireland into which it would be introduced, however, was not at all receptive to this new bill. Public opinion, influenced by the ongoing propaganda of the republican organisations, the continuing arrests under

●

Below: An anti-conscription postcard from 1918. (Kilmainham Gaol Museum)

FIRST IRISH CONSCRIPT.

the Defence of the Realm Act and the ongoing hunger strikes, as well as high-profile deaths such as that of Thomas Ashe, had swung towards Sinn Féin. Despite internal wrangling for power and position, by early 1918 the party was in pole position to influence Irish opinion on this very real threat of conscription—and it wasn't the only organisation determined to oppose its introduction. Conscription was, as Senia Paseta notes, 'the greatest and final unifying issue in pre-independence nationalist Ireland'. On this single issue the IPP and Sinn Féin temporarily put aside their many differences and stood as one in opposition, while the Catholic Church was also opposed to it, on the basis that the Irish had not given their consent to the war in the first place. Crucial to the anti-conscription campaigns, however, would be the trade union movement and the women's organisations. Once the Military Service Bill was passed by the Commons, all those opposing individuals, groups and organisations sprang into action. Within three days (18 April) a united front of all shades of trade unionism, feminism, nationalism and republicanism was coming together to campaign against it. As well as Sinn Féin, the IPP and the Catholic Church, those who actively opposed conscription included the Labour Party, Cumann na mBan, the Irish Citizen Army, the Irish Women Workers' Union (IWWU) and the Irish Volunteers.

An all-party conference called by the lord mayor of Dublin, Lawrence O'Neill, at the Mansion House on 18 April agreed a Sinn Féin pledge that declared that conscription was 'a declaration of war on the Irish people', and all present swore to 'resist conscription by the most effective means at our disposal'. The Church hierarchy also agreed to this, although they demanded that the so-called 'effective means' should be within the letter of the law. As Townsend noted, this 'fusion of clerical and political leadership transformed Irish politics'. The Catholic Church could provide an effective framework of mass mobilisation—the pulpit and the parish network. With

the backing of the Church, Sunday 21 April was a day of anti-conscription activism, fund-raising, incendiary speech-making and pledge-signing outside churches in parishes, towns and villages across the country, with priests stating that they would 'lead their people to death, sooner than accept conscription'. Hundreds of thousands signed the pledge, over £250,000 was collected for the Defence Fund, and a surge of new membership of the Irish Volunteers, Sinn Féin, Cumann na mBan and other nationalist organisations was noted around the country.

Other 'most effective' methods of resistance were provided by the trade union movement, the Labour Party and the women's organisations. On 20 April a special meeting of the Irish Trade Unions Congress (ITUC), attended by about 1,500 members, affirmed Ireland's right to self-determination and called for a general strike against conscription. This general strike, which happened on 23 April in all parts of Ireland except north-east Ulster, gave practical effect to the resolutions passed by Sinn Féin, the IPP, the Irish Volunteers and the Catholic hierarchy. Outside of Ulster it was hugely successful: pubs, shops, railways, newspapers and factories closed, and all transport ground to a halt. Organised and led by the unions and the Labour Party, the strike shut down much of the country while, despite a ban, almost every town and city had marches. At City Hall in Dublin, thousands converged to sign the anti-conscription pledges. Interestingly, women, organised by the IWWU and Cumann na mBan, took their own pledge, which included the promise not to 'fill the places of men deprived of their work through enforced military service'. Irishwomen were not going to be the supportive 'home front' if their men went off to war. So stunning was the success of this strike that the *Irish Times* noted that 'April 23 will be chiefly remembered as the day on which Irish Labour recognised its strength'. It was, as Townsend notes, 'the final nail in the coffin of the conscription project'.

This mass mobilisation of

resistance brought an end to any active attempts to impose conscription, but also engendered an intensification of repression from the authorities. In May, after Lord French was appointed lord lieutenant, some

> **This mass mobilisation of resistance brought an end to any active attempts to impose conscription, but also engendered an intensification of repression from the authorities.**

73 prominent Sinn Féiners were arrested under the DORA, charged with conspiring with Germany (the so-called 'German Plot') and deported to prisons in England. French, who was willing now to accept 50,000 'volunteers' in lieu of conscription, also initiated a coercive recruitment campaign. Resistance to this continued from all the groups who had rejected conscription. Drawing on its pre-1916 experience of running anti-recruitment campaigns, Cumann na mBan, for example, organised flag days, with the slogan 'Women won't Blackleg', and anti-conscription meetings. As one of the largest, and growing, advanced nationalist organisations in the country, it had the expertise to organise another national event of resistance. 'Lá na mBan' (Women's Day) was a major, all-Ireland anti-conscription event which took place on 9 June 1918 and which involved thousands of female activists from several organisations. Women collected signatures; the *Freeman's Journal* reported that 40,000 had signed the anti-conscription pledge in Dublin's City Hall alone. Over 700 uniformed Cumann na mBan members, who, 'from the spectacular point of view, provided the leading feature of the day's proceedings', were present at City Hall. More spectacularly, over 2,400 IWWU

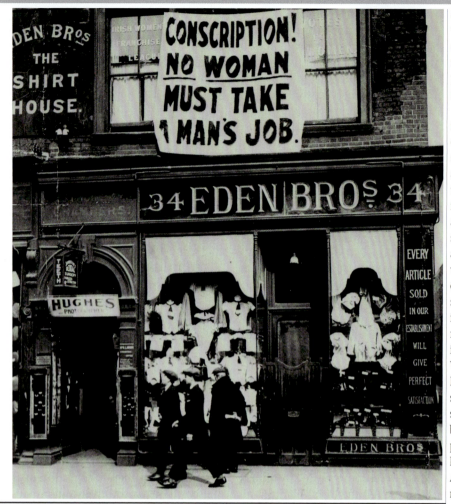

women who 'made the biggest show' also marched to City Hall. The campaign included a 'solemn pledge for the women of Ireland', signed by an estimated two thirds of Ireland's women, which stated that 'the enforcement of conscription on any people without their consent is tyranny'.

Despite the continuing arrests and repressive measures, including in July 1918 the proscribing of nationalist organisations, public demonstrations and meetings, as well as the imposition of extreme censorship on newspapers, the anti-conscription campaigns had been successful. Conscription was never enforced, and results of the coercive recruitment drives of the summer of 1918 were dismal for the British authorities. They had hoped for 50,000 recruits, but fewer than 10,000 men joined up. While the threat of conscription was not finally lifted until after the

armistice in November 1918, it was effectively dead in the water by late April/early May of that year. More disastrously, however, from a British perspective was that the anti-conscription campaigns served to heighten nationalist fervour throughout the country, with popular opinion swinging behind republicanism. Membership of the Irish Volunteers, Cumann na mBan and Sinn Féin surged. The moderates, those who would have been expected to support constitutional nationalism, were by now swinging towards Sinn Féin. The beginning of the end of the IPP was in sight, especially as the Catholic Church swung its support towards a greener shade of nationalism. For Labour, April and the general strike would prove to be a high point. In the December 1918 general election, Labour was more a passive bystander than a contender, and in that moment ceded leader-

ship to the resurgent and ultimately victorious Sinn Féin. It was to have, as Arthur Mitchell wrote, the 'most serious consequences both for the party and for the labour movement' into the future.

The failure to quiet the country in the aftermath of the Rising, the ongoing repressive measures and sweeping arrests into 1917–18, which alienated much of the population, the propaganda effects of the Ashe funeral and the politically unwise attempt, in 1918, to extend conscription to Irishmen meant that the atmosphere in Ireland was growing very volatile just as Britain was ending its war in Europe. The conscription crisis was a minor, if irritating, episode for a British government more concerned with America's entry into the war and with events on the Western Front. For Irish republicans, however, now emboldened by their success in the campaign against conscription and their numbers enlarged by the confinement of hundreds in prisons, 'the universities of the revolution', it was a propaganda coup. Anti-conscription had proved the most successful mass mobilisation of civil disobedience in the years after 1916. It galvanised a sizeable portion of the population, especially younger people, who were now more attracted to the republican cause.

Mary McAuliffe lectures in Gender Studies at University College Dublin, specialising in Irish women's social and political history.

Further reading

M. McAuliffe & L. Gillis, *Richmond Barracks 1916—we were there: 77 women of the Easter Rising* (Dublin, 2016).

S. Paseta, *Irish nationalist women, 1900–1918* (Cambridge, 2013).

C. Townsend, *The Republic: the fight for Irish independence, 1918–1923* (London, 2014).

M. Ward, *In their own voice: women and Irish nationalism* (Cork, 2001).

Above left: An anti-conscription banner on the offices of the Irish Women's Franchise League, *c.* 1916, urging women not to fill roles in the workplace that might be vacated by conscripts into the British Army. (Getty Images)

IRELAND AND THE GERMAN *REVOLUTIONSPROGRAMM* AFTER 1916

BY **JÉRÔME AAN DE WIEL**

From the German plot that was (1917) to the German plot that wasn't (1918).

'[No]. It is better that a cankering sore like this should be cut out', was Captain Reginald Hall's reply to Casement when the latter pleaded, on Sunday 23 April 1916, to be allowed to contact certain people in Dublin to call off the planned rising. Hall was the leader of the ultra-secret Room 40, located in the Admiralty building in London. Thanks to a series of extraordinary pieces of luck, British naval intelligence was already able to decrypt German codes during the opening months of the war. In other words, it knew pretty much everything there was to know about the planning of the Easter Rising. Karl

Spindler, the German captain of the *Aud* which was to bring 20,000 rifles to the Irish Volunteers, found it amazing that he was not stopped once by the Royal Navy on his way to Tralee Bay. He thought: 'Our luck in this respect began to seem a little uncanny. Could there be something behind it? Did the British know about our coming?' The answers to his two questions are both yes. Spindler was eventually cornered by the Royal Navy off the Irish coast. The rising went ahead on Monday 24 April and resulted in about 450 deaths, 2,600 wounded and the destruction of Dublin city centre. Hall wanted to protect his invaluable German source, and preventing the rising at the last minute might have alerted the Germans to the fact that something might be wrong with their codes. But this was not

the main reason. Hall calculated that the rising would provide the British with a golden opportunity to get rid of disloyal Irish elements. The Irish Volunteers were poorly armed, so the security risk would be minimal. The subsequent carnage told a different story.

But this was not the end of German intrigue in Ireland. On 8 September, Clan na Gael leader John Devoy again approached the German ambassador in Washington, as he had done for the planning of the Easter Rising, and submitted a memorandum to him, explaining that the events in Dublin had fired up the Irish people and that the *Aud*'s unfortunate gunrunning attempt had nevertheless shown Germany's goodwill to Ireland and proven that the Imperial Navy could reach the Irish coast: 'We ask that as large a quantity of arms, ammunitions and equipment and as strong a military force as the German Government feels it can send be dispatched to a point or points in Ireland …'. It was stressed that 250,000 men would participate in a second rising, that the Germans would be able to set up submarine bases in Ireland—notably at Foynes, where there was 'an enormous quantity of petrol'—and that 'the same reasoning applies to bases for Zeppelins …'. The German embassy sent their coded messages to Berlin, and Room 40 decrypted away. In Berlin, the Germans probably knew that some passages in the memoran-

THEY ARE AWAITING "THE DAY"

Non-Commissioned Officers of 'The Irish Brigade' in Germany who discarded the red and donned the Green.

●

Left: Non-commissioned officers of Roger Casement's Irish Brigade who participated in the German plot. (Joseph McGarrity Collection, Villanova University)

CONSCRIPTION

SIR EDWARD CARSON: "Frankly, I'm not all round your neck but everybody wants me to marry you for your Conscription Dowry."

Vote for McCARTAN AND NO CONSCRIPTION.

Printed for the Candidate, Doctor Patrick McCartan, by O'Loughlin, Murphy and Boland, Ltd., Dublin; and published by the Sinn Féin Election Committee, 6 Harcourt Street, Dublin.

IRISHMEN SHOULD BE DEFENDED!

New York, July 12, 1918.

Fellow-Citizens:

Several Irishmen have been arrested and held for trial on various charges on account of their connection with Irish affairs.

Liam Mellows, Dr. Patrick McCartan and Seumas McDermott have been charged with obtaining passports irregularly. Thomas Welsh is charged with carrying letters as a means of communication between men in this country and the men in Ireland.

Jeremiah A. O'Leary is awaiting trial for Treason, and his brother John is being tried as this appeal is written on a charge of aiding his brother in fleeing from the jurisdiction of the Court.

John Gill, a man whose son is at the front in France, has been held incommunicado for several weeks without any charge being made against him, denied the right to communicate with his sick wife and constantly intimidated to compel him to give evidence against Jeremiah O'Leary, which he solemnly declares he cannot give. And now he is committed for contempt of court for refusing to testify before the Grand Jury.

The guilt or innocence of these men will be established before the courts and when their cases are presented they will no doubt be given a fair and impartial trial. But they need able lawyers to defend them, and the first trial of John O'Leary has revealed the fact that intimidation is being practiced to prevent lawyers from taking up the cases of Irish citizens charged with connection with "Plots." The newspapers have frequently stated, on the authority of officials of the Department of Justice, that numerous arrests of Irish citizens are to be made throughout the country on charges of complicity in a "German-Irish Plot," which every intelligent Irishman knows does not exist. Here we have the evidence that war is being waged on the Irish National Movement on the pretence that it is hostile to the United States.

It is therefore necessary to insure a fair trial for every Irishman charged with complicity in this alleged Plot; and this can only be done by providing them with able counsel and the other necessary expenses of a trial. To accomplish this a large amount of money is necessary, and it must be raised by voluntary subscriptions.

A legal defense fund has been started in New York to defray the necessary expenses to insure these men a fair trial and make certain that all their legal rights are safeguarded. The undersigned have been selected as a disbursing committee.

This is an appeal which should recommend itself to the Friends of Irish Freedom and other kindred organizations, and we ask you to take the matter up with your organization and solicit subscriptions. The case is urgent, as we are called upon to pay heavy expenses at once.

Checks and Post Office orders should be made payable to Matthew G. Lyons, 1064 Third Avenue, New York.

JOHN DEVOY, *Chairman.*
JOHN KENNY, *Secretary.*
MATTHEW G. LYONS, *Treasurer.*

dum were wildly exaggerated. They wrote '?!' in the margin next to the passage about the Zeppelins.

Nonetheless, it did not take them long to agree to organise a second gunrunning operation and they had very good reasons for doing so. Germany's strategic position was not particularly brilliant. The offensive at Verdun had been a bloody failure and the British and French armies had launched their own offensive on the Somme, the two battles resulting in several hundreds of thousands of casualties. Moreover, the German population was feeling the effects of the blockade imposed by the Royal Navy; food supplies were running short. To the mind of many a decision-maker in Berlin, Britain was in fact the *Hauptfeind* (main enemy), as it was thought that she would fight or

● Above: This election poster for Sinn Féin candidate McCartan in Armagh demonstrates the extent to which conscription was an election issue. (NLI)

● Above right: A letter written by John Devoy to help fund-raise for the 'German plot'. (NLI)

finance the war until the bitter end. Destabilising Britain through Ireland therefore made sense, and the IRB, Irish Volunteers, Irish Citizen Army and Clan na Gael had shown that they meant business.

But Ireland was also part of the wider German *Revolutionsprogramm*, a strategy that consisted in destabilising the Triple Entente's empires and territories by fomenting revolution. The failed Easter Rising and the future successful Russian Revolution had the common point of having been actively supported by Berlin. In December the German admiralty and general staff eventu-

ally agreed on the following. Two steamers equipped with guns and carrying 60,000 rifles, twenty machine-guns and twelve million rounds would leave for Ireland; one landing would take place in Galway and another one in Tralee. No soldiers would be sent, although it had initially been envisaged. Submarines and the laying of sea-mines would protect the landing of the arms. A precise date was set for the landings, 21 February 1917. This was an ambitious large-scale operation.

On 16 January 1917, however, the German embassy in Washington sent a coded message to Berlin that cancelled the operation. Devoy had been in contact with a man called Liam Clarke (if that was his real name) in Ireland. Clarke had been wounded in the GPO in 1916 but had managed to avoid arrest. He had told Devoy that he had seriously overestimated the strength of the Volunteers, who were still being reorganised. There was also some dissatisfaction regarding Germany's support for the Easter Rising, but the main point was that no German soldiers would participate in *Aufgabe P*, which meant that a second rising had no chance of success. Room 40 appreciated the information and eventually warned Dublin Castle on 17 February that the Germans would attempt a large-scale gunrunning operation between 22 and 25 February. Room 40 omitted to say, however, that the operation had been *cancelled*. Instead, an arrest list of 27 republicans, Irish Volunteers and Sinn Féiners was drawn up. It included Seán T. O'Kelly, T.J. McSweeney, Dr P. McCartan and Darrell Figgis. The arrests were made on the night of 21 February, the night the Germans were supposed to arrive but didn't. Hall's approach was the same as for the Easter Rising: to his mind it was a similar golden opportunity or pretext to decapitate the republican movement.

Aufgabe P was the last serious German involvement in Ireland, although in October an Irishman called Ryan approached the German ambassador to Switzerland to ask whether the Germans 'could support a possible rising on 7 November with an action on Ireland's west coast'. The request was transmitted to the supreme army command and the admiralty but the latter was not remotely interested: 'Once again, the old Irish story. The Irish are unreliable people whom one should not trust.' The matter ended there.

But as the old French saying goes, *jamais deux sans trois* (never two without three). After the Easter Rising in 1916 and *Aufgabe P* in 1917, the conscription crisis in 1918 provided Hall with another opportunity to decapitate or to keep leader-less the Irish republican movement. In April 1918, David Lloyd George made the worst decision ever in the long and troubled Anglo-Irish relationship by imposing compulsory military service on Ireland. Despite having received advice to the contrary, the 'Welsh Wizard' knew better. As could have been easily predicted, his decision had the effect of uniting Sinn Féin, the Irish Parliamentary Party, Irish Labour and the people. This extraordinary alliance was led by the Catholic Church, which rejected the authority of the Westminster parliament. It was a velvet revolution and the government's conscription plan was squarely defeated.

At that time the Germans had decided to send a man to Ireland by submarine. His name was Joseph Dowling, from Roger Casement's ill-fated Irish Brigade. Some aspects of Dowling's mission are still unclear but he was captured on 12 April and declared to his captors that he had come to discuss a German gunrunning plan and landing. Lord French wrote: 'I didn't believe a word of it'. It is indeed most unlikely at this stage of the war that the German high command would have focused its attention on Ireland. That it was a scaremongering operation meant to divert more British troops from the Western Front seems a much more plausible explanation.

In any case, the British cabinet agreed that British law and order should be restored in Ireland. On 9 May 1918, it decided that all Sinn Féin leaders who had contacts with the Germans should be arrested. On 17 May the authorities arrested more than 80 Sinn Féiners, among them Éamon de Valera, Arthur Griffith and Countess Constance Markievicz. The people were incensed and Sinn Féin gained in popularity. Hall claimed that he had 'absolutely reliable' proof of Sinn Féin's involvement with the Germans but that it could not be divulged as his sources needed to be protected.

The episode went down in history as the 'German Plot', but even Lord Wimborne and General

Bryan Mahon were not convinced that the British authorities had a case. Today, in the archives of the Foreign Office in Berlin and the Federal Military Archive in Freiburg in Breisgau, there is no trace or hint whatsoever of any German conspiratorial moves in April/May 1918. Hall had probably used the evidence he had for 1916 and 1917 to justify these arbitrary arrests. There was nothing for 1918. The new bishop of Limerick, Dr Denis Hallinan, called it a 'British plot'. He was right, but could not have known *how* right he was.

Jérôme aan de Wiel lectures in modern European history in University College Cork.

Further reading

J. aan de Wiel, *The Catholic Church in Ireland, 1914–1918: war and politics* (Dublin, 2003).

J. aan de Wiel, *The Irish factor, 1899–1919: Ireland's strategic and diplomatic importance for foreign powers* (Dublin, 2008).

C. Townshend, *The Republic: the fight for Irish independence, 1918–1923* (London, 2014).

Above: After the failure of the Rising, John Devoy (1842–1928) continued to seek international support for Irish independence. (NLI)

THE LIVES OF OTHERS

'Despite the Rising's repercussions, ordinary life continued in 1917, and two new influences began their inexorable rise: the GAA and the film industry. In the background, however, perhaps the greatest of all catastrophes was about to strike: the Spanish 'Flu epidemic.'

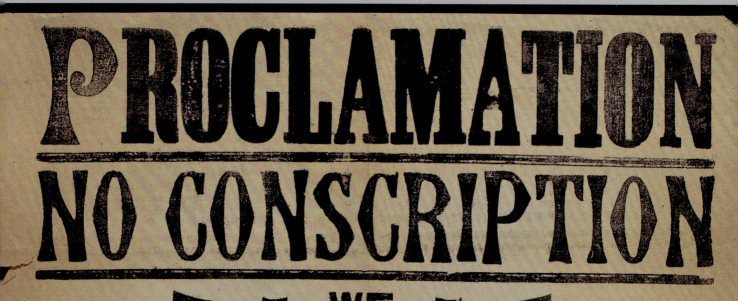

Image: A poster for an anti-conscription 'Aerideacht' organised by Cumann na mBan in County Roscommon, 1918, complete with athletics competition. While the GAA is not directly referenced, the event points towards how participatory activities such as sports, and sporting venues, could be harnessed to attempts to secure popular support for political causes. (NLI)

'A discontented and rebellious spirit is widespread'.

THE RADICALISATION OF THE GAA AFTER 1916

BY **RICHARD McELLIGOTT**

A black mourning rosette adorned fifteen blue and gold jerseys as the Tipperary hurlers walked onto the field to face Limerick on Sunday 25 June 1916. This simple gesture in honour of the martyrs of 1916 was greeted with cheers from the large crowd. The match, part of a tournament to celebrate the centenary of the Christian Brothers in Limerick city, took place on the first weekend since the Rising that Gaelic games had been permitted to be played.

Ever since martial law had been proclaimed during the Rising all sporting events had been strictly prohibited. Yet with summer slipping away and the events of Easter now two months old, the GAA was increasingly anxious to resume its sporting programme. Successful lobbying by Irish MPs resulted in the British authorities finally withdrawing their restrictions on GAA activity in late June. The Tipperary hurlers would go on to win the 1916 All-Ireland (the final was delayed until January 1917). Making their way through the fire-gutted ruins of Sackville Street to Croke Park that morning, the team stopped outside the shelled façade of the GPO and recited a decade of the Rosary in memory of those who had fought and died there.

Such tokens of remembrance and commemoration were now increasingly common occurrences at GAA events. In Ulster, clubs had already begun to rename themselves after the leaders of the Rising. By June 1916, RIC reports were showing that nationalist opinion was displaying a growing empathy with the rebels' cause, and GAA matches pro-vided some of the earliest occasions for this. Soon the RIC were noting that 'a discontented and rebellious spirit is widespread [which] frequently comes to the surface at Gaelic Athletic Association tournaments'.

This was perhaps unsurprising. Politically the GAA was seen by many of its supporters and detractors as an avowedly nationalistic body. The association and its leadership certainly considered themselves pillars of the Irish-Ireland movement, and it was largely the products of that cultural reawakening of the 1890s that had led the recent revolt against British rule. There was no denying the fact that in the years before 1916 key members within the GAA had flirted with radical nationalism. In 1911 the future president of the association, Dan McCarthy, told a meeting of members that he wanted GAA men 'to train and be physically strong [so that] when the time comes the hurlers will cast away the camán for the steel that will drive the Saxon from our land'.

Likewise, many prominent officials were well-known members of both the Irish Republican Brotherhood and the Irish Volunteers. In Kerry the local GAA, under the leadership of Austin Stack, was centrally involved in the plans to land and distribute German weapons to aid the uprising in Dublin. In other areas, such as Wexford and Galway, players and officials in the association were conspicuous in the events there both before and during the Rising. In Dublin itself, 302 GAA members from 52 separate clubs were numbered among the 1,500 rebels who fought in the city that Easter. While the GAA did not enjoy a sporting monopoly among the rebels, it was by far the most heavily represented sports body among them.

●

Below: Harry Boland on the pitch in Croke Park, 1919. Boland was prominent in the GAA, the Irish Volunteers, the IRB and Sinn Féin. While genuinely committed to the association, he also recognised its value to the independence movement. (NLI)

● Above: Waterford's Young Ireland Hurling Club, October 1916, presumably around the time they drew the county senior final with Ferrybank Shamrocks. They lost the replay the following November. (NLI)

● Opposite page: A Sinn Féin postcard, with a hurl prominent against the backdrop of a republican flag and a variety of weapons. (NLI)

But the association was first and foremost a sports organisation. While many may have viewed membership of the GAA as an affirmation of their cultural and political outlook, for many more politics was, at best, a secondary concern to their sporting passions. Before the Rising, the vast majority of those members who were politically inclined would have described themselves as constitutional nationalists who fully supported the cause for Irish Home Rule. In this the association merely reflected the political opinions of wider Irish society. The three years following the Rising, however, would see the GAA and its broad membership become increasingly politically radicalised.

Following the Rising, the British authorities conducted a campaign of harassment against the GAA on both a local and a national level. Hundreds of ordinary members were among the 3,400 arrested and deported for their supposed involvement in the failed Rising. Owing to the numbers of players interned in camps like Frongoch, Gaelic football contests became an important part of prisoners' daily lives. They were arranged to keep up the discipline, fitness and morale of the men. Internment now brought many GAA members face to face with the emerging radical political doctrine being developed in these 'universities of revolution'. As William Mullins, an internee and footballer with the Tralee Mitchels GAA club, stated:

'I am fully convinced that Frongoch made our whole organisation into what it eventually reached. The comradeship that developed in Frongoch and the knowledge we got of each other from different parts of the country … was a binding force in the future. John Bull made an awful blunder when he put us all together there.'

The arrest and detention of their comrades had also begun to harden GAA members' views of the British government. The emergence of Sinn Féin as a political mass movement in 1917 would play a crucial role in the radicalisation of the association. The RIC's inspector general was forced to admit that there was now a widespread belief among the Irish population 'that one week of physical force did more for the cause of Ireland than a quarter of a century of constitutional agitation'. The increasing reality for many was that political freedom from Britain could be achieved more quickly by adopting the policy of defiance advocated by groups like Sinn Féin rather than the old Irish Parliamentary Party policy of co-operation.

Many adherents of Sinn Féin within the GAA used their influence to help indoctrinate members into the movement and there was now a significant correlation between local GAA and Sinn Féin membership. By May 1917 Sinn Féin's popularity was said to be so great that it 'virtually dominated' the association. In June 1917 the British government commuted the sentences of all those still held after the Rising. Among those released to heroes' welcomes at home were Thomas Ashe and Austin Stack, two leading figures in the Irish Volunteers and IRB with strong GAA connections. In the weeks that followed, Stack and Ashe toured Ireland, imploring young men to reform the Volunteers while also eulogising Sinn Féin, the organisation that had politically benefited most from their imprisonment.

In Clare, the county board began the process that saw Éamon de Valera nominated to contest the by-election for Sinn Féin in July. That same year the Clare footballers would reach the All-Ireland final, entering their matches under a banner proclaiming 'Up de Valera'. Meanwhile, prominent GAA officials such as Stack and the Dublin GAA president Harry Boland were appointed onto Sinn Féin's ruling executive. The association also hoped to capitalise on the new patriotic spirit enflaming Irish public opinion. Its central council issued letters to county boards to reform clubs that had gone out of existence 'and take advantage of the present feeling throughout the country by establishing such clubs with the object of wiping out soccer and other foreign games'. Likewise the GAA began to support and run competitions in aid of the

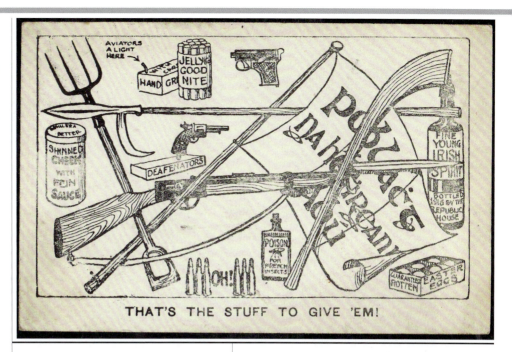

THAT'S THE STUFF TO GIVE 'EM!

Irish National Aid and Volunteers' Dependants' Fund, set up to provide monies to families of those killed or imprisoned after the Rising. In February 1917 a special GAA sub-committee, chaired by Boland, was established to organise a national tournament for the fund. The association soon became its principal source of finance.

In August 1917 Stack and Ashe were arrested for making seditious speeches. In protest they and other republican prisoners in Mountjoy jail began a hunger strike, which resulted in Ashe's death five days later. Nationalist public opinion in Ireland was outraged. Those within the GAA were similarly appalled by the death of their former member. The Dublin county board issued a damning statement 'deploring the killing' and resolving to have representatives of every GAA club in the city at the funeral. Ashe's martyrdom was the catalyst for a huge expansion of the Sinn Féin movement across Ireland. By December it was reported that the party now had over 1,000 branches and 66,000 members. The rising tide of Sinn Féin nationalism did not lift all GAA boats, however. In Louth, the *Dundalk Democrat* bemoaned the fact that local GAA matches were now seemingly nothing more than Sinn Féin

demonstrations.

When in the spring of 1918 the British government made its fatal attempt to extend conscription to Ireland, a special meeting of the GAA's central council unanimously declared: 'That we pledge ourselves to resist by any and every means in our power the attempted conscription of Irish manhood'. Huge public demonstrations were held across Ireland to resist conscription, while an enormous uptake in enlistment in the reorganised Irish Volunteers was recorded. This had the natural effect of feeding large numbers of GAA members into the Volunteers. In areas like north Kerry it was reported that hurling matches were being used to mask the convening and drilling of several local Volunteer contingents.

Faced with growing political unrest, emergency rule was imposed on Ireland and all public gatherings and political rallies were banned. These rules were framed to include GAA events. Within a week, matches in several counties were being broken up, as local RIC patrols baton-charged the assembled crowds. Outraged over the government's interference with its games and emboldened by the mass protests that had defeated the attempt to introduce conscription into Ireland, the GAA now began to

•
Above: The Dublin (Collegians) team that won the 1917 GAA All-Ireland hurling title. They beat Tipperary (Boherlahan) by 5-4 to 4-2 in the final, played in Croke Park on 28 October 1917.

orchestrate its own peaceful mass protest.

The GAA ordered all county boards to organise an extensive programme of matches to be held across every county on Sunday 4 August 1918. This mass protest of games, dubbed 'Gaelic Sunday', initiated a trial of strength between the government and the GAA. At 3pm, nearly 1,800 matches took place in almost every county in Ireland. The newspaper *Sport* reported that as many as 4,000 teams and 60,000 players participated, and practically every affiliated GAA club in the country was involved. Faced with such mass disobedience, the authorities were powerless. The success of the event put an end to the British government's direct interference with the GAA. Gaelic Sunday represented the largest, most widespread and most successful act of public defiance against British rule in Ireland in the 1916–

22 period. It forcefully demonstrated the association's growing belligerence towards the British administration on the island.

With Sinn Féin's resounding success in the 1918 general election, the GAA now began to align itself firmly within the broader nationalist movement headed by that party. Having been elected leader of Dáil Éireann following his escape from prison in April 1919, de Valera received a rapturous reception from the 25,000-strong crowd attending the final of the GAA's Volunteers' Dependants' Fund tournament at Croke Park. That same month the association pushed through laws to expel from its ranks Irish civil servants who had been required under new rules to take an oath of allegiance to the king. For the best part of fifteen years the GAA had banned members of the RIC and the British military from its ranks. This new ban on the likes of teachers and office clerks showed how the GAA was now using itself directly as a weapon against the British state in Ireland. Those in control of the association were employing a form

of 'social ostracism', long advocated by Sinn Féin, against sections of their own membership whom they saw, by their employment, as contributing to the British administration in Ireland.

In view of such policies, there can be little doubt that by 1919 the GAA had taken an increasingly radical position and had in effect become an active opponent of British rule in Ireland.

Richard McElligott lectures in modern Irish history in University College Dublin.

Further reading

R. McElligott, 'The GAA, the 1916 Rising and its aftermath to 1918', in G. Ó Tuathaigh (ed.), *The GAA and revolution in Ireland: 1913–1923* (Cork, 2015).

R. McElligott, *Forging a Kingdom: the GAA in Kerry, 1884–1934* (Cork, 2013).

W. Murphy, 'The GAA during the Irish Revolution, 1913–23', in M. Cronin, W. Murphy & P. Rouse (eds), *The Gaelic Athletic Association 1884–2009* (Dublin, 2009).

The twentieth century was the century of mass death and yet, contrary to popular misconception, the greatest killer of all time was neither Hitler nor Stalin but an illness often mistakenly associated with the common cold—epidemic influenza.

GREATEST KILLER OF THE TWENTIETH CENTURY

BY **GUY BEINER, PATRICIA MARSH AND IDA MILNE**

As the First World War was entering its final stages, a pandemic of unprecedented virulence, which we now know to have been the H1N1 influenza virus, infected one billion people around the globe and may have killed approximately 100 million. It spread with remarkable speed, striking in three almost simultaneous waves in various parts of the world. It initially appeared in the late spring and summer of 1918. It then returned in full strength in the autumn and early winter of that year, and reappeared for a final deadly bout in the early months of 1919. The helplessness of the medical profession (which only discovered that influenza was a virus two decades later) punctured their new-found confidence in bacteriology to combat disease.

It was misnamed 'Spanish influenza' because newspapers in neutral Spain freely reported on the epidemic (including the illness of King Alfonso XIII), unlike the belligerent states, which suppressed news reportage in order not to demoralise the war effort. Although its provenance remains uncertain, a disease with similar symptoms was documented among British troops during the winter of 1916 in Étaples and Aldershot. Current research, however, highlights the outbreak in

US military cantonments in March 1918 and suggests that it may have spread from there through military and civilian transport networks.

In the absence of any one effective medicine or vaccine, doctors used a broad range of treatments for the symptoms of influenza. These included calomel (as a purgative), oxygen, stimulants, including strychnine, salicylates, quinine, trional or some preparation of opium for sleeplessness, gargles prepared from a tincture of creosote or a solution of permanganate of potash, cough remedies and linseed poultices. Punch made from hot water, sugar and whiskey was prescribed to relieve pain and alleviate breathing difficulties. Whiskey was also used as a prophylactic. Over-the-counter panaceas added influenza to the list of ailments they claimed to cure. Phosferine, advertised as a cure for war-inflicted nervous disorders, now claimed to cure 'flu. Bovril and Oxo were alleged to fortify the body against the onslaught of disease. Dublin's only homeopathic pharmacy, Hanna's, advertised gelsemium as a cure for 'flu. Ultimately, the best weapon against the disease was bed rest and good nursing.

It is often said that the pandemic killed more people than the Great War, which had an estimated death toll of ten million. Although

this is true globally, it was not the case from a regional perspective, as European war casualties outnumbered the over two million estimated influenza fatalities across the continent. In Ireland, 20,057 people were reported as having died of influenza in 1918 and 1919 (the average annual rate for the preceding years of the war had stood at 1,179). In addition, an increase in deaths caused by related illnesses, most notably pneumonia, from which over 3,300 died above what would have been usually expected, can be attributed to the epidemic.

Sir William Thompson, the registrar general, admitted that the official influenza mortality rate was a conservative estimate, and there are reasonable grounds to assume that additional influenza deaths in Ireland were uncertified, attributed to other illnesses or simply not recorded at all. The overall number is probably lower than fatalities of Irish servicemen in the First World War but exceeds deaths in the War of Independence and the Civil War.

Applying to official mortality figures an estimate that only 2.5% of those who caught influenza actually died suggests that there were

> **Whereas influenza mortality is typically high among the elderly and the very young, a global peculiarity of the 1918–19 pandemic was its targeting of normally healthy young adults.**

over 800,000 influenza cases in Ireland, 20% of the population. Between June 1918 and April 1919 the epidemic, which further taxed a health service already struggling with war-related shortages of medical personnel and hospital beds, temporarily incapacitated urban and rural communities across the island.

The first wave, which hit Ireland

● Left: Catherine Moran aged sixteen, *c.* 1910—she later married Lance Corporal Charles Heatley (above) of the Royal Dublin Fusiliers, who was killed on the first day of the Battle of the Somme in 1916. She died in November 1918 from influenzal pneumonia in her parents' house in Nicholas Street, with her three young sons at her bedside. (NAI)

first wave, Leinster and Ulster were the worst affected. The almost equally severe third wave, which lasted from mid-February to mid-April 1919, affected Dublin again, as well as the western part of the island (in particular Mayo and Donegal). As influenza moved through towns and communities, schools, libraries and other public buildings were closed and court sittings postponed. Businesses closed sporadically on account of staff illnesses. Medical officers of health, mainstays of the Poor Law medical system, worked around the clock to treat their patients, paying 100,000 more home visits during the epidemic than in the previous year. Hospitals and workhouse infirmaries struggled to cope with the numbers of patients, pharmacists worked long hours to dispense medicines, and mortuaries, undertakers and cemeteries had to queue the dead for burial.

Some areas suffered severely during all three waves, notably Dublin, where troops returning from

in the early summer of 1918, was the least destructive, although severe enough for schools and businesses to close. The earliest verifiable record of its arrival in Ireland can be found in US naval archives, which document an outbreak on the USS *Dixie*, docking outside Queenstown (Cobh), in May 1918. From 12 June the *Belfast News-Letter* reported that

Belfast had been struck by an influenza epidemic, and by the end of June there were reports that it had reached Ballinasloe, Tipperary, Dublin, Derry and Cork. Nevertheless, by mid-July the first wave had abated.

The second wave, from mid-October to December, was the most virulent of the three and, as in the

the war may have been a major factor. Dublin county and borough had an influenza death rate of 3.7 per thousand living (1,767 'flu deaths) in 1918 and of 2.3 per thousand living (1,099 deaths) in 1919. At 3.85 per thousand Belfast had one of the highest influenza death rates in 1918, but in 1919 it had one of the lowest—0.79 per thousand. Some counties almost escaped the epidemic. Clare, for example, had the lowest death rate from influenza of any county in 1918, at 0.46 per thousand. Kildare had the highest influenza death rate in 1918—3.95 per thousand (263 deaths). Water and power shortages in Naas during the height of the second wave contributed to a particularly severe local outbreak in the county.

Whereas influenza mortality is typically high among the elderly and the very young, a global peculiarity of the 1918–19 pandemic was its targeting of normally healthy young adults. In 1918, 22.7% of all deaths from influenza in Ireland were of people aged between 25 and 35, and in 1919 the figure for this age group was 18.95%. The registrar general estimated that there were more male than female deaths from influenza in Ireland, which contrasted with the rest of the United Kingdom, where slightly more female than male deaths were recorded. Ulster followed the British pattern, as the female influenza mortality was

slightly higher than the male, especially in the more industrial areas of the province. There were high proportions of women textile workers in Belfast, Derry, Lurgan and Lisburn, and the overcrowded, hot, damp conditions of linen workshops encouraged the spread of influenza. In Belfast, females between 25 and 35 had the highest influenza mortality of any other age or gender group in the city.

Individuals employed in occupations involving close contact with the general public were more likely to contract influenza. Doctors and nurses were particularly exposed. The high number of Dublin teachers suffering from influenza in October 1918 led to the closure of schools in the city. Absence owing to influenza depleted police forces throughout Ireland. Public transport employees were also vulnerable, and in Belfast 100 tramway employees were absent with influenza during July 1918 and 120 in November. Priests and clergymen were also in the front line, and a lot of them died. Staff illness forced the closure of shops, with many shopkeepers and assistants dying.

In a curious coincidence of history, the epidemic in Ireland became intertwined with the fate of the DORA prisoners incarcerated in Belfast Jail on short-term sentences and with the mass arrests and internment of Volunteers and Sinn Féin members in relation to the

alleged 'German Plot'. Newspaper reports that over 100 Sinn Féin prisoners in Belfast Jail had contracted influenza during October 1918 prompted questions in parliament as to their treatment. Arthur Samuels, attorney general for Ireland, dismissed Sinn Féin allegations of neglect and claimed that special treatment and diet were provided and that two extra doctors had been engaged to assist in the prison. Fionán Lynch, one of the inmates, attributed the prisoners' preferential medical treatment to Sinn Féin's highly efficient propaganda, as the British authorities wanted to avoid the negative publicity that would follow prisoner deaths. Ironically, with not a single fatality among the prisoners, Belfast Jail seemed to be the safest place in the city during the epidemic.

The Irish internees held in Usk Prison, Monmouthshire, were not as fortunate. Six prisoners at Usk fell victim to 'flu in late November but were not provided with regular access to a doctor until 1 December. The death of Richard Coleman from Swords on 9 December bolstered Sinn Féin's allegations of prisoner mistreatment. The timing of Coleman's death was opportune: the general election was to be held on 14 December. Newspaper coverage of the circumstances of his death and Sinn Féin's orchestration of his funeral procession through the streets of Dublin bought the party valuable publicity. Frank Gallagher, assistant in Sinn Féin's propaganda department, maintained that it turned the tide of public opinion by influencing undecided voters to vote Sinn Féin.

The shortage of medical personnel led to calls from many boards of guardians for the release of three German Plot internees—Doctors Richard Hayes, Bryan Cusack and H. Russell McNabb—to do 'flu duty (the three were subsequently elected Sinn Féin MPs), and for Dr Kathleen

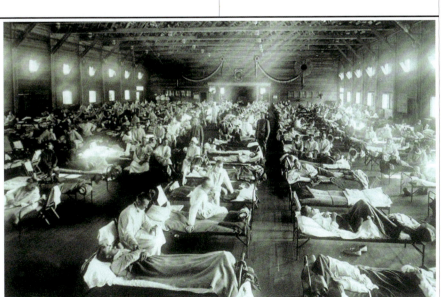

Left: Emergency influenza hospital at Camp Funston, Kansas, USA, in 1918. (National Museum of Health and Medicine, USA)

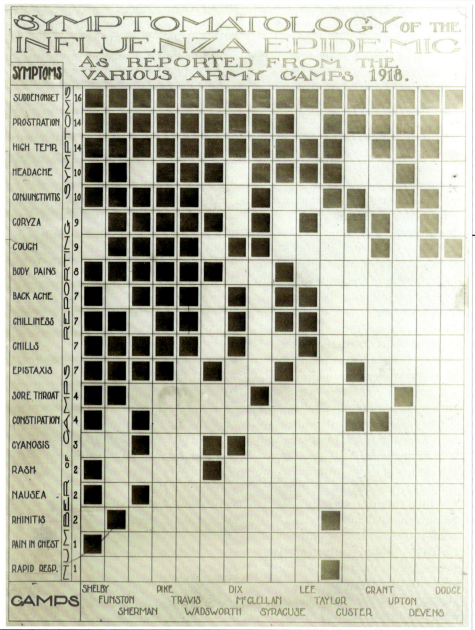

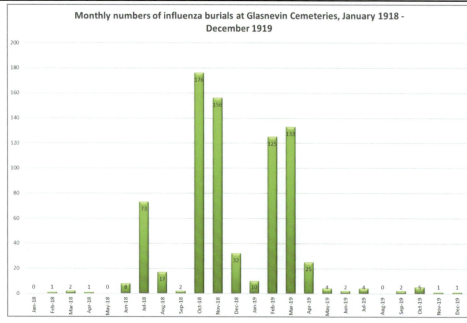

● Left: Chart outlining the symptoms of influenza from the US Army Department in 1918. Demobilised soldiers were often affected, and huge movements of populations after the war created problems for disease control. (Otis Historical Archives National Museum of Health & Medicine)

● Below left: Chart showing monthly numbers of burials at Glasnevin Cemetery in Dublin, January 1918–December 1919. This reveals the peaks in the outbreak that occurred in the city, reflecting wider pandemic patterns, and shows the pressure that the cemetery would have been under to bury the many dead. (Glasnevin Trust)

Lynn, who managed to evade the initial round-up, to be permitted to come off 'the run' to treat 'flu victims. Lynn was arrested for a few hours on 31 October 1918 and was released on condition that she work with the ill during the crisis. She set up a vaccination centre and hospital for 'flu victims at Charlemont Street.

The epidemic did not reach Reading Jail, where many of the leaders were detained, but during the third wave several prisoners contracted influenza at Gloucester Jail. Arthur Griffith tried to lift the spirits of the younger sufferers by fighting the 'flu on his feet, self-medicating with large quantities of quinine (which may have contributed to the health problems that led to his early demise). The death of Tipperary East MP Pierce McCan on 6 March 1919 was thought by many to have persuaded the authorities to order a general release of the Irish internees held in British jails (though in fact the orders had been signed on 4 March).

Summing up the local effects of the epidemic in its immediate aftermath, Sir William Thompson noted that 'Since the period of the Great Famine with its awful attendant horrors of fever and cholera, no disease of an epidemic nature created so much havoc in any one year in Ireland as influenza in 1918'. Surprisingly, however, it has not featured in Irish historiography. The ground-breaking documentary *Aicíd*, screened on TG4 in November 2008, was the first programme to introduce the topic to public debate in Ireland.

The 1918–19 pandemic poses a paradox for world history. Killing more people in a fifteen-month period than any other calamity of similar duration, it could be considered one of the greatest catastrophes of all time. Remarkably, however, it has been mostly forgotten. In contrast to the worldwide large-scale commemoration and memorialisation of the First World War, there are no museums, heritage centres, exhibitions, national monuments or remembrance days dedicated to the pandemic. Unlike the extensive cultural memory of the Great War, the Great 'Flu has barely had a passing mention in literature. Edvard Munch's self-portrait is one of the few works of art on the subject. No epic feature films depict the ravages and human suffering caused by the pandemic. Memory was mainly confined to private spheres, and the personal grief for lost loved ones, long recalled in family traditions, was not vented in public.

There are many possible reasons that could explain this social amnesia. Globally, the Great 'Flu was overshadowed by the upheaval of the Great War, while political turmoil in Ireland during this period may also factor in why it has been omitted from Irish historiography. It was a passing episode—striking suddenly and then just as mysteriously disappearing. Social psychology shows that memory is often founded on schemata or templates of earlier memories, but, unlike other diseases, influenza was not lodged in popular memory as a cause of terror. Moreover, high politics dominated history writing at the time and influenza did not kill prominent national figures. While it is possible to politicise a natural disaster, the global dimension of the pandemic overruled incrimination of local villains (despite Irish republican attempts to finger Perfidious Albion). In recent years, however, recurring threats of outbreaks of new influenza

●

Right: Contemporary Ernest Noble cartoon— 'Good evening, I'm the new influenza'. (Welcome Library, London)

pandemics have reawakened general interest in the Great 'Flu of a century ago.

Guy Beiner is a senior lecturer at the Department of History in Ben-Gurion University of the Negev, Israel. Patricia Marsh completed her Ph.D at the School of History and Anthropology, Queen's University Belfast, in 2010. Ida Milne is an Irish Research Council Marie Curie Elevate fellow at Maynooth University.

Further reading

N. Johnson, *Britain and the 1918–19 influenza pandemic: a dark epilogue* (Abington and New York, 2006).

P. Marsh, 'The war and influenza: the impact of the First World War on the 1918–19 influenza pandemic in Ulster', in D. Durnin & I. Miller (eds), *Medicine, health and Irish experiences of conflict, 1914–45* (Manchester, 2016).

I. Milne, 'Stacking the coffins: the 1918–1919 influenza pandemic in Dublin', in L.M. Griffith & C. Wallace (eds), *Grave matters: death and dying in Dublin 1500–2000* (Dublin, 2016).

H. Phillips & D. Killingray (eds), *The Spanish influenza pandemic of 1918–19: new perspectives* (London and New York, 2003).

An earlier version of this article first appeared in HI 17.2 (March/April 2009).

A-TICH-OO!!

GOOD EVENING I'M THE NEW INFLUENZA!!

The years 1916–18 were a key period in the integration of cinema into Irish society.

FILM:
A NEW FORM OF PROPAGANDA AND ENTERTAINMENT

BY **DENIS CONDON**

In the early 1910s speculative capitalists, taking advantage of the growing international trade in moving-picture entertainment, had produced a building boom in the construction of picture-houses. These new entertainment venues appeared not only on the streetscape of cities and large towns, where theatres and other entertainment venues had always been located, but also in suburbs, small towns and villages, where professional entertainment had never before been offered on a regular basis. With that substantial infrastructure in place, the later war and post-Rising years were particularly notable for the various struggles to use and control it.

Before the war, governments, political parties, the churches and other dominant social institutions had mostly ignored cinema or had tried to suppress what they initially saw as a pernicious working-class fad. During the war, however, powerful interests began to recognise cinema's value. As the cinema boom grew on the back of increasing middle-class interest in the business opportunity and in film as a new form of entertainment, cinema was taken more seriously.

Some of the difficulties that the authorities may have had in taking cinema seriously are suggested by the fact that the first big film star was comedian Charlie Chaplin, who began his film career with the California-based Keystone Company in December 1913. It was not so much the fact that he was a comedian that made Chaplin difficult to assimilate for those in power but that his comedy so consistently took the perspective of the underclass—so iconically represented in his 'tramp' persona—against those placed above

●

Opposite page: A photograph of the Picture House, Sackville/O'Connell Street, taken during the week of 8–13 May 1916. (RTÉ Archives)

●

Below: Charlie Chaplin look-alike contests happened around the world; this image from the one held in Dublin is from 1916. (*Film Fun*, January 1916)

him in the social hierarchy. Although Chaplin by no means either invented this field or had it to himself, he had become popular so quickly that less than a year and a half after his first appearance on Irish screens in June 1914 Irish cinema owners were holding competitions for the best Chaplin imitators. Cathal MacGarvey, well-known entertainer and manager of Dublin's Masterpiece Theatre, filmed the contestants of the Chaplin competition he held in September 1915 and had the audience choose the best screen performance.

This kind of activity in picture-houses offers a sense of how the cinema culture of the 1910s differed from later forms. Although this level of audience participation was rare, some kind of live performance inviting audience interaction almost always accompanied the programme of films offered. The most common live portion of the entertainment was musical accompaniment of the silent moving pictures either by a single pianist or violinist or by an orchestra of a size dependent on the prestige of the picture-house. Featured musicians playing solos, singers or variety performers sometimes also appeared between films. The number of films that constituted a programme varied, but by the late 1910s it most often included a long dramatic feature film with a star actor supported by a combination of shorter comedies,

episodes of serial films, factual films, cartoons and newsreels.

Despite the anti-establishment potential of elements of the programme, the interests of picture-house owners and film producers were in regularising their industry in line both with the regulations of local and national government and

> **Before the war, governments, political parties, the churches and other dominant social institutions had mostly ignored cinema or had tried to suppress what they initially saw as a pernicious working-class fad. During the war, however, powerful interests began to recognise cinema's value.**

with the attitudes accepted by a large swathe of the middle class. As the 1910s progressed, picture-houses became larger and more luxurious, employed uniformed attendants and

A NEW FORM OF THE CHAPLIN CRAZE

In Ireland they term Charlie Chaplin the greatest cinema comedian in the films. The management of a picture house in Dublin held a competition for Chaplin imitators, of which there are hundreds. Each entrant was required to give an impersonation before a camera. When all had done so, the film was shown in the Dublin theater, and the audience was asked to pick the winner.

offered more comfortable seating to higher-paying patrons. Film-makers vied for the rights to adapt popular and high-brow literary works and lured star actors from the theatre with unprecedented salaries. Trade organisations attempted to self-regulate to avoid imposed censorship. In Ireland, the Catholic Church-based Irish Vigilance Association introduced a Catholic nationalist flavour to the censorship campaign by suggesting that the London-based British Board of Film Censors (founded in 1912) was not sufficiently attuned to the needs of Ireland's largely Catholic population.

Although the outbreak of war brought hardships of various kinds to the film industry, not least the interruption of international trade, it also offered opportunities for cinema to show its social utility. Films were shown at recruiting events in Ireland from 1915, and in April 1916 H. Higginson resigned managership of the newly reopened Clontarf Cinema in Dublin to lead a cinema recruiting campaign. He proposed to give two shows in each place the campaign reached, the first exhibiting army and navy films, and the second offering a regular drama and comedy programme whose proceeds would go to various war funds.

Nevertheless, the British government did not overcome its scepticism about the production of official war films until early 1916. At that point, urged on and aided by the industry-founded British Topical Committee for War Films (BTCWF), it began making propaganda films, among the most successful and best remembered of which is *The Battle of the Somme* (1916). '[F]rom the moment of preparation, all through that deadly, but glorious, First of July, on to the crash of victory,' the *Belfast News-Letter* commented of this feature-length factual film released to enormous success in September 1916, 'the story is unfolded in all the strength and simplicity which such photography can give.'

This sense of the communicative potential of cinema was echoed in the opening article in the inaugural January 1917 issue of *Irish Limelight*, Ireland's first cinema trade journal and fan magazine. '[N]o other medium can provide the man who has something to say with so receptive and so enormous an audience,' it argued. In the 1910s, many Irish men and women had something to say, among them nationalists, unionists, suffragists and labour activists. Although films had been made in Ireland since cinema's earliest days, they had largely been made by foreign companies visiting the country and generally reflected an outsider's perspective. Even when local speculators saw the opportunities represented by building picturehouses and exhibiting films to local audiences, very few cultural producers attempted to make films. Those who did faced several challenges. Ireland had little film-making expertise; the increasingly

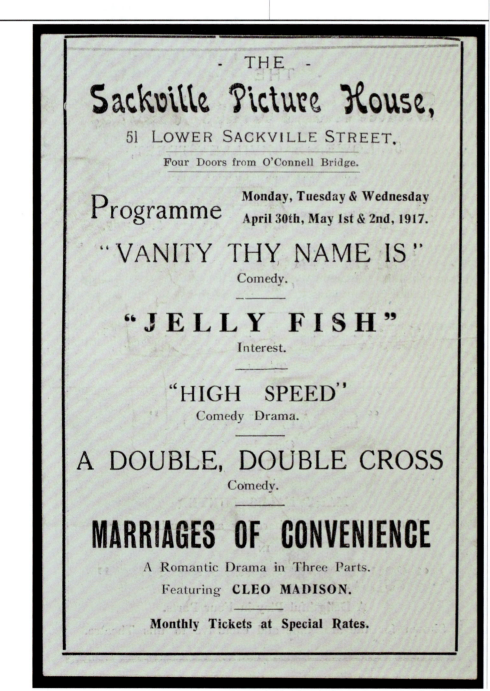

● Left: The listing for the Sackville Picture House on Sackville Street, 1917. (NLI)

● Opposite page: The silent film *Birth of the Nation* was shown in the Gaiety Theatre in September 1916. (NLI)

dominant feature film was expensive to make and required the participation of at least one well-known actor; the most successful films were those that could appeal to an international audience rather than offering culturally specific content; and the system of distribution was increasingly controlled by powerful international companies.

Nevertheless, the 1916–18 period is remarkable for the appearance of indigenous fictional and factual film companies that faced these challenges. When Irish-American diplomat James Mark Sullivan and Irish businessman Henry Fitzgibbon founded the Film Company of Ireland (FCOI) in March 1916, it was not the country's first fiction production company but it would become the most significant one of the 1910s. Sullivan and Fitzgibbon aimed to use Irish actors and writers to revise the misrepresentation of Ireland by foreign film-makers. Despite the destruction during the Rising of its initial Dublin offices at 16 Henry Street, the company went on to make nine short dramas and comedies in 1916, all of them directed by Abbey Theatre actor J.M. Kerrigan and featuring actors from the Abbey and other theatres. None of these films survives, but FCOI's far more ambitious *Knocknagow* (1918), an adaptation of Charles J. Kickham's novel, does still exist. Directed by Abbey actor and manager Fred O'Donovan in the wake of Kerrigan's departure to America, this consciously conceived national epic was shot at Tipperary locations associated with Kickham and his novel in the summer of 1917 and released in Ireland in early 1918. FCOI's films were popular in Ireland, but its limited success abroad caused financial problems that meant that it made just one other feature film, *Willy Reilly and his Colleen Bawn* (1920), before the company folded in 1920.

Although Norman Whitten's General Film Supply (GFS) had been making cinema advertisements and films of local events since its foundation in May 1913, it began to produce 'Irish Events'—the first indigenous newsreel—in July 1917. Newsreels or topicals, which typically consisted of five one-minute stories of recent events, were provided by the British companies who produced the popular Pathé Gazette, Gaumont Graphic and Topical Budget, and all of these did occasionally cover Irish stories. English-born Whitten occasionally sold his films of newsworthy events to these companies, but in July 1917 he formalised GFS's local film-making into the weekly Irish Events, to which many Irish picture-houses subscribed. Irish Events filmed many of the key political and social events of the period, including the funeral of Thomas Ashe, Sinn Féin's election victories and the first Dáil. As well as providing the weekly newsreel in its five-minute format, GFS also offered a growing number of newsreel specials, generally focusing on one topic and running for ten minutes. A 1918 advertisement of its specials featured *Irish Sinn Féin*

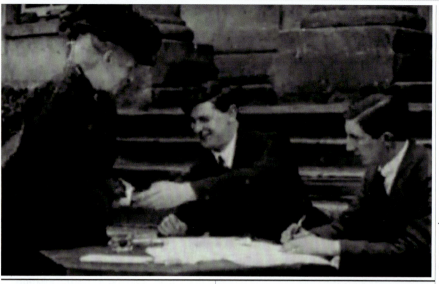

Convention; *Funeral of Thos. Ashe*; *Release of the Sinn Féin Prisoners*; *South Armagh Election*; *Consecration of the Bishop of Limerick*; *Funeral of the Late John Redmond, M.P.*; and *Waterford Election*. 'It has been proved,' boasted the advertisement, 'that topicals such as any of the above will attract a larger audience than a six-reel exclusive.'

Newsreel companies including GFS made films in Dublin at the time of the Rising that appear to suggest that it represented a set-back for cinema. In *Easter Rising, Dublin 1916*, the camera spends some time examining the ruined façade of the iconic DBC restaurant on the east side of Lower Sackville (now O'Connell) Street before panning past the substantially destroyed building beside it and across the smoking ruins of the rest of the block to the corner of Lower Abbey Street. The building

next to the DBC was the Grand Cinema, opened by hotelier William Kay in 1913 as the second of the four picture-houses—along with the Sackville Picture House (1910), the Pillar Picture House (1914) and the Carlton Cinema (1915)—that would operate on Sackville Street in the 1910s. Kay did not rebuild the Grand but instead entered a joint management arrangement at the prestigious Rotunda Pictures with journalist and printer James T. Jameson, who since the early 1900s had made the Rotunda at the top of Sackville Street the base for the countrywide operations of his Irish Animated Picture Company.

Despite all other utopian plans and speculations, when Dublin actually emerged from the ruins of 1916 it did so as a cinema city. The DBC itself would be replaced by the Grand Central Cinema (1921), a picture-house with approximately 1,000 seats—four times as many as the Grand—and the Grand Central would almost back on to the equally large Corinthian Cinema (1921), which would replace three destroyed buildings on Eden Quay. Larger again were the 1,500-seat Metropole Cinema (1922) and the 3,200-seat La Scala Theatre (1920) on ruined sites adjacent to the GPO. The La Scala's siting on the former premises of the *Freeman's Journal* and of publisher Alex Thom—as well as Jameson's change from print to cinema—are indicative of the wider shift in media that was under way.

Denis Condon lectures in Irish cinema at Maynooth University.

Further reading

D. Condon, *Early Irish cinema, 1895–1921* (Dublin, 2008).
Early Irish Cinema (blog), 2013–17.

●

Above left: Michael Collins, always alert to propaganda opportunities, seized the opportunity to film a public signing of Dáil Loan documents at the by now significant location of St Enda's.

●

Left: The Carlton Cinema, one of four cinemas operating on Sackville Street in the early part of the twentieth century.

THE VICTORY OF SINN FÉIN

'On 14 December 1918 the election that changed Ireland forever took place. The Irish Parliamentary Party (IPP or Home Rule party), the dominant force in Irish nationalism for over a generation, was swept away in a landslide for Sinn Féin. The party that under John Redmond had thought itself on the verge of finally winning self-government was now reduced to just six out of 105 Irish seats.'

Image: Éamon de Valera and others pictured on the steps of Ennis Court House for the Clare elections on Wednesday 11 July 1917. (NLI)

One way to interpret the Irish political metamorphosis of 1916–18 is to examine the usurpation, transformation and radicalisation of the Sinn Féin party. The second is to look towards the declining potency and popularity of the Home Rule movement and the slow failure of its leader and chairman, John Redmond.

THE DECLINE AND FALL OF THE REDMOND EMPIRE

BY **CONOR MULVAGH**

JOHN REDMOND   485-14

Was the decline of the Home Rule movement crisis-driven or systemic? In 2005 the historian Michael Wheatley neatly parsed this question by asking whether the party was 'representative' or 'rotten' on the eve of the First World War. The challenge presented to the historian of post-insurrection Ireland is to determine to what extent the Irish Party remained viable before its decimation in the December 1918 general election. The by-elections held between Rising and Armistice present mixed messages. If the somewhat chaotic and anomalistic Cork West by-election of November 1916 is included, the tally stands at five victories for the Irish Parliamentary Party (IPP) and five for Sinn Féin, with three of the Irish Party's victories having occurred in the spring of 1918.

To understand the decline of the IPP, it is essential to understand the nature of the party's leadership. John Redmond, the chairman of the party from its reunification in 1900 until his death in March 1918, ruled with the consent and assistance of John Dillon, the sometime leader of the majority faction of the IPP during the split of the 1890s. In Redmond's inner circle were two other allies of Dillon: T.P. O'Connor and Joseph Devlin. Devlin was the sole member of the post-1900 influx to the party who was singled out for elevation. By the end of the first decade of the twentieth century, it was universally agreed among Redmond, Dillon and O'Connor that Devlin would be their heir apparent and the favoured successor to Redmond when transition was deemed necessary.

This model of collaborative leadership was never static, but from 1900 it proved effective in managing a political machine that was truly global and utterly modern for the politics of its day. The leadership was no monolith and the internal tensions and alliances within this group had an influence on the direction of party policy and the efficacy of the movement both in Ireland and at Westminster. Upon the outbreak of the Rising, the Irish Party leadership was geographically divided, with Redmond and O'Connor in London, Devlin in Belfast and Dillon in Dublin. The latter differed from Redmond in his reaction to the Rising and revisited his misgivings over recruitment and Irish nationalist support for the war effort, which had become a defining element of Redmond's outlook and vision for a Home Rule Ireland since 1914.

In terms of the Irish question, the 1916 Rising resulted in a redoubling of Downing Street's efforts to put the Home Rule question to bed once and for all. Lloyd George, then minister for munitions in the Asquith coalition cabinet, was tasked with finding a solution for Ireland acceptable to all parties. He took up where all parties had left off in July 1914 at the Buckingham Palace Conference. This time, however, rather than round-table deliberations, he opted for proximity talks, negotiating with unionists and nationalists separately.

Lloyd George had been informed by Lord Northcliffe, a close friend of T.P. O'Connor's, that Devlin had expressed the opinion that an immediate settlement for Ireland was of paramount importance following

Opposite page: John Redmond, chairman of the Irish Parliamentary Party from 1900 to his death in 1918, pictured in the US in 1908. (Library of Congress)

the Rising. This was the signal the government needed to embark upon an effort to reach consensus towards the resolution of the Irish impasse. O'Connor reported to John Redmond that Devlin held private misgivings about negotiation and was distrustful of British intentions following the stalled conference of 1914. As if Devlin's hesitation was not bad enough, Redmond was also facing a muted rift with Dillon. In a letter to O'Connor on 20 May 1916, Dillon admitted that he differed 'profoundly' from Redmond on the way forward.

Dillon was not averse to settlement but felt that it would have to fall to others to find room for compromise. He confessed to O'Connor: 'It is I am convinced much better for me not to be in London—at the time of the first Conference between Redmond and Asquith—as I am almost certain I should feel compelled to dissent and object—it is far better to leave the field clear to those who believe that a workable arrangement is possible'.

Thus the summer 1916 negotiations went ahead with a desperate Redmond, a reluctant Devlin and an absent Dillon. Of the fourth member of the inner leadership, his biographer, referring to him at a slightly later period, notes that O'Connor 'showed every sign … of being enthralled by Lloyd George's performances'. It is generally understood that O'Connor was mesmerised by the soon-to-be prime minister and was precariously straddling his nationalist allegiances and his Liberal Party social circle.

With this somewhat grim outlook, the Lloyd George negotiations proceeded. By late June, Devlin had been brought more firmly on side, especially through the encouragement of O'Connor. The settlement offered by Lloyd George at that point was for the immediate enactment of Home Rule for 26 counties only, and the continued attendance of Irish MPs at Westminster for the duration of the war. Once the European conflict had ended, an

imperial conference would convene to hammer out a final settlement for Ulster. The six north-eastern counties would, in the interim, remain under direct rule from Westminster and outside the remit of the proposed Irish Home Rule parliament.

With this offer on the table, Joseph Devlin was cautiously on board. Redmond immediately capitalised upon Devlin's acceptance of the terms on offer. With Redmond and Dillon both in tow, Devlin was encouraged to speak at an assembly of the Ulster delegates of the United Irish League in Belfast on 23 June 1916. At this watershed convention, Devlin delivered a 45-minute speech urging Ulster nationalists to get behind Lloyd George's scheme.

●

Above: Redmond's close ally T.P. O'Connor MP on a fund-raising tour of the US in 1917. (Library of Congress)

●

Right: A pre-war propaganda postcard opposing Home Rule. The proposed permanent exclusion of six Ulster counties from any Home Rule arrangement remained unacceptable to the IPP and continued to dog their negotiations with the British government.

Despite Devlin's private hesitancy about the policy for which he was advocating, he nonetheless threw himself into the task of convincing the delegates. Following his speech, the convention voted 475 to 265 in favour of the Lloyd George scheme, approving the temporary partitioning of their province for the safeguarding of national Home Rule.

Having made Herculean efforts to sway opinion in nationalist Ulster, Devlin had entered into something of a Faustian pact. In the time that elapsed between the Ulster nationalist vote and the presentation of the scheme to parliament, unionists within Cabinet intensively lobbied both the prime minister and Lloyd George. Austin Chamberlain and Lord Lansdowne appear to have been the two most effective petitioners, convincing Asquith and Lloyd George to engage in an act of cloaked duplicity: agreeing to make exclusion permanent and also sanctioning the immediate removal of Irish MPs from Westminster. This proposed Balkanisation of the Irish problem likely appealed to both Asquith and Lloyd George, who were keen to allow the cabinet to divest itself of Irish concerns and focus its full attention on the war.

On 10 July 1916, a barbed question from Carson in the House of Commons forced Asquith to put the government's altered position on the public record. The IPP was predictably furious at this betrayal. On

22 July Redmond was formally informed that the cabinet had indeed assented to permanent six-county exclusion and the removal of Irish MPs from Westminster. This was final confirmation that all of Devlin's hard work in Belfast had been spectacularly demolished. Devlin was ill at the time, but when he returned to parliament at the end of the month he informed the Commons that 'If I ever march through the division lobbies again ... it will be for the purpose of clearing the present coalition Government out of power ... I would never agree to the permanent exclusion of Ulster'.

A.C. Hepburn succinctly summarises the feeling within the party at this point. Dillon wrote privately that these negotiations 'struck a deathblow at the Irish Party', while then MP for Galway City Stephen Gwynn later ventured that 'that day [22 July] really finished the constitutional party and overthrew Redmond's power'.

Hepburn notes that the mishandling of the 1916 talks exposed Lloyd George's fallibility as a political negotiator. It did not, however, impede his ascension to the prime ministry, as he replaced Asquith in December 1916. The desire to get on with the war was central to the outlook of the new administration. Lloyd George's design for Ireland was to outsource the problem, leaving it to a representative body of Irishmen to solve the question amongst them-

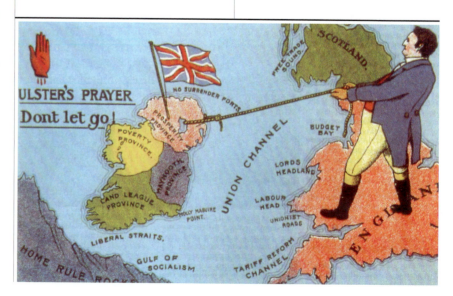

selves. In the wake of the failed 1916 negotiations, Asquith had written a personal note to Redmond encouraging him to 'keep the "negotiating" spirit alive'. Dillon, and now Devlin, had grown averse to negotiation, but Redmond, imbued with Asquith's conciliatory spirit, came to see himself as the custodian of negotiation within the party. When the idea of an Irish 'convention' was floated, Redmond threw himself enthusiastically into the scheme.

Devlin had mellowed somewhat since his outburst to the Commons in July 1916. As the idea for an Irish Convention began to take shape in May 1917, he was prevailed upon to accede to his chairman's wish to attend as a delegate. Just as in the Lloyd George negotiations, Dillon was adamant that he would not personally be involved in the Irish Convention and calculated that its membership would be packed in favour of both Ulster and southern unionists.

As the composition of the Convention was being finalised, Dillon wrote to T.P. O'Connor, who was by then on a North American party fund-raising tour. He sardonically counselled O'Connor not to be 'too enthusiastic about [the] Convention, or put all your money on its success'. Underlining the dissonance of their opinions, Redmond would later proudly proclaim to the opening assembly of the Convention that 'for the first time … Ireland has been asked … to settle these problems for herself'.

Sinn Féin's abstention from the Irish Convention meant that the emerging radicalism of nationalist Ireland had no voice there. In a society on the cusp of major franchise extension and the seemingly inevitable reinvention of post-bellum politics, the Irish Convention rapidly began to resemble what modern pundits might call an echo chamber. In this artificially constructed cross-section of Irish society, the Ulster unionists had disengaged and Sinn Féin was absent. Even the voices of less conciliatory constitutional nationalists like Dillon were not present. Thus southern unionists

MR. JOSEPH DEVLIN, M.P.
AND THE
IRISH BRIGADE

" May every good fortune, success and blessing attend the colours of the Irish Brigade, whose valour, I hope, will be crowned with the laurels of glory worthily earned in the arena of a great conflict on behalf of a righteous cause . . . . .

" When they come back again, they will be welcomed not only as soldiers of the Allies, but as friends of liberty who have raised the dignity and prestige and glory of Ireland to a higher position than it ever occupied before . .

IRISHMEN
DO YOUR DUTY IN THIS RIGHTEOUS CAUSE AND
JOIN THE IRISH BRIGADE

5,000. WLP.661, 3/6. HELY'S LIMITED, DUBLIN

received a prominence far outweighing any real-world political clout they then possessed. Meanwhile, various methods were employed in attempts to manufacture consensus among the Convention's diverse membership. Ultimately, Redmond found himself drifting from the concerns of his grass roots while trying to find common ground at Regent House with unlikely bedfellows such as the London-born Munster land magnate Viscount Midleton.

In November 1917 Stephen Gwynn warned Redmond that Dillon was leading other nationalist conventioneers away from Redmond's camp. Gwynn admitted: 'I fear, as too often happens, Dillon and not you will shape the line. Dillon has more tenacity and more persistence and by these qualities he has again and again … prevailed against your larger and wiser judgement.'

The Irish Convention returned

●

Above: A recruiting poster quotes Joe Devlin in support of the war effort. (Library of Congress)

from its Christmas recess to thoroughly transformed circumstances. Redmond had failed to carry the support of Devlin into the New Year and he learned on 15 January that neither Devlin nor the Catholic bishop of Raphoe—a firm Home Ruler—would stand by him in supporting Midleton's scheme. Devlin had finally had enough of concilia-

tion. The Christmas break had allowed him to step back from the Convention and perceive its increasing futility in the face of rapidly changing political realities in the real world.

While many consider his death to be the end of his chairmanship, John Redmond's leadership had ceased to be tenable shortly before

his untimely demise on 6 March 1918. On 26 February, Redmond wrote to Dillon relinquishing the chairmanship and leaving it to Dillon and Devlin jointly to decide upon the question of succession. While this underlines the selflessness that was a hallmark of Redmond's political career, it also exposes the reality of failure that rested upon his legacy as he awaited the surgeon's knife in the spring of 1918.

Returning to Wheatley's conundrum of whether the IPP was representative or rotten, analysis of post-insurrection politics shows that Lloyd George's duplicity can be construed as a deathblow to the already struggling party: the potency of Redmond's leadership was weak going into the Irish Convention and had virtually evaporated by February 1918. Wheatley has observed that, within the broad church of constitutional nationalism, Redmondism had always been a 'minority taste'. As Redmond's position mutated in reaction to the outbreak of the war, the shock of the Rising and the hopeless position in which he found himself at the Irish Convention, however, to what extent had the flavour of Redmondism changed, and when did his supporters finally discover that Redmondism had become unpalatable?

Conor Mulvagh lectures in Irish history at University College Dublin.

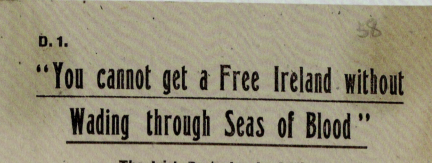

D. 1.

"You cannot get a Free Ireland without Wading through Seas of Blood"

—The Irish Party Leaders' View of Irishmen fighting for the Freedom of Their Own Country.

Their Views of Irishmen "wading through seas of blood" for England are different.

MR. JOHN DILLON, in the English House of Commons, May 11th, 1916, speaking of the Men of Easter Week, said:—

"I am proud of their courage, and if you were not so dense and stupid as some of you English are you could have them **FIGHTING FOR YOU....** (Hon. Members: "You stopped them.") That is an infamous falsehood. I and the men who sit around me here have been **DOING OUR BEST TO BRING THESE MEN INTO THE RANKS OF THE ARMY."**

MR. JOSEPH DEVLIN, speaking in the English House of Commons, April 9th, 1918, said:—

"There was not a Sunday for nearly two years that I did not stand on Irish platforms . . . appealing to the sense of chivalry, the love of liberty, and the fighting spirit of our race **TO TAKE THEIR STAND. THE RESPONSE WAS MAGNIFICENT."**

". . . . Some of the Irish regiments were cut to pieces, and there was hardly a man left alive."

—John Dillon, House of Commons, April 10th, '18.

On their very own showing, was not the Irish Party the Party which shed seas of Irish blood? No less than 60,000 Irishmen have been mutilated and slaughtered in this war—FOR WHAT? Who are Dillon and Devlin, to traduce the Sixty-Eight Men who Died in Easter Week?

Further reading

A.C. Hepburn, *Catholic Belfast and nationalist Ireland in the era of Joe Devlin, 1871–1934* (Oxford, 2008).

R.B. McDowell, *The Irish Convention, 1917–18* (Oxford, 1970).

C. Mulvagh, *The Irish Parliamentary Party at Westminster, 1900–18* (Manchester, 2016).

M. Wheatley, *Nationalism and the Irish Party: provincial Ireland 1910–1916* (Oxford, 2005)

●

Left: A Sinn Féin pamphlet from 1918 invokes the Easter Rising to castigate the Irish Party for their support for the British war effort, quoting Devlin in the process. The unpopularity of the war was increasingly used as a stick with which to beat the IPP after 1916. (NLI)

'The very badge of serfdom'—press censorship, 1916–18.

DUBLIN CASTLE AND THE PRESS AFTER THE RISING

BY **IAN KENNEALLY**

To better understand the press in Ireland in the years after the Easter Rising, we need to return, briefly, to August 1914 and the outbreak of the First World War. That month, amidst public fears of secret plots and German espionage, the British government had moved quickly to enact the Defence of the Realm Act (DORA) with the stated aim of 'securing the public safety'. Press clauses were a significant part of the legislation and DORA made it a court-martial offence to publish 'false reports or make false statements; or spread reports or make statements intended or likely to cause disaffection to His Majesty or to interfere with the success of His Majesty's forces'. In order to suppress reports that might cause 'disaffection' (a deliberately vague term), the Act gave the authorities the power to search newspaper offices or to seize and dismantle machinery.

But what of the press that was being censored? Who were the leading newspapers and what was their reach among the Irish population? The *Irish Independent* had a circulation of over 100,000 copies per day, but its main competitor and bitter enemy in the daily market was the *Freeman's Journal*, a paper that was effectively an arm of the Irish Parliamentary Party until 1919. The circulation of the latter, whose offices near the GPO had been destroyed during the Rising, lagged far behind that of the *Independent*—certainly under 50,000 copies, and probably around 35,000 copies. The *Irish Times*, seen within and outside Ireland as the voice of southern unionism, had a circulation comparable to, or slightly higher than, the *Freeman's Journal*, while weekly regional newspapers such as the *Westmeath Independent* may have sold 10,000–20,000 copies per edition.

Press censorship applied to the newspaper industry as a whole but, given that the mainstream press was largely supportive of the war effort, the authorities expected little trouble from that quarter. Indeed, shortly after the outbreak of the war, Dublin Castle judged only one regional newspaper, the *Meath Chronicle*, to be potentially troublesome. The British administration was mainly concerned with republican and labour newspapers, and the nature of the Irish press at this time can be gauged from an intelligence note to the chief secretary's office in late 1914. Surveying the press landscape, the writer of the memo noted only 'seven papers of doubtful loyalty': *Éire, Fianna Fáil, Irish Freedom*, the *Irish Volunteer, Sinn Féin*, the *Irish Worker* and the *Leader*.

Each of these seven papers had their offices raided by the military, with the result that 'three stopped publication of their own accord, two were and have remained sufficiently in order not to warrant seizure [the *Leader* and the *Irish Volunteer*], and

●

Above left: William Martin Murphy, founder and owner of the *Irish Independent*. (RTÉ Stills Library)

two have been dealt with'. By 'dealt with', the author meant that the papers had been suppressed under DORA. This censorship was highly effective in quieting the one recalcitrant section of the press, although experienced journalists such as Sinn Féin's Arthur Griffith would make creative efforts to circumvent the restrictions. Another consequence of these suppressions was that they encouraged newspapers to work within the state-imposed confines of DORA. The acquiescence of the Irish press with the stipulations of DORA can be seen in the fact that the British Press Bureau, which oversaw censorship, had not, during 1914 and 1915, assigned anyone to concentrate specifically on Irish newspapers. The shock of the 1916 Rising, however, caused the British government to institute a much harsher censorship regime in Ireland.

By the end of May 1916, Dublin Castle had created an Irish press censorship office headed by John Beresford, Lord Decies. From then on all Irish newspaper editors were asked by the government to provide proofs of their copy to Decies. The proofs were generally provided after publication and each newspaper's content was examined in Decies's office for material that contravened DORA. In some instances, particularly for labour or republican papers, editors were required to send their proofs before publication. Decies would then judge what could and could not be printed. Frank Gallagher, a Sinn Féin journalist and later editor of the *Irish Press*, detailed in his memoirs how republicans attempted to slip proofs of articles and reports past Decies by distracting him with discussions of horse-racing and the excessive levels of income tax, topics in which Decies had an obsessive interest. Another tactic was to overwhelm Decies with unacceptable proofs in the hope that some would go unnoticed. While Gallagher wrote of the 'great game', it was not a game in which most of the press indulged, since newspapers could not afford to risk the wrath of the Castle administration and the loss of income that suppression would bring.

Although a number of republican and labour newspapers were suppressed immediately before and after the Rising, the *Enniscorthy Echo* was the first mainstream paper to be suppressed during this period. Owned and edited by William Sears, a member of Sinn Féin, the paper had come to be regarded by the authorities as the most republican of the regional press. A contributory factor in its suppression was that a number of the *Echo*'s staff, including Robert Brennan, who later worked on the *Irish Bulletin*, were Volunteers and had participated in the Rising. A handful of regional newspapers were suppressed during the second half of 1916, including the *Kerryman* and the Tralee *Liberator* in August 1916. In the case of the *Kerryman*, the military party who enforced the suppression handed the editor a notice stating that his paper had recently published an article 'calculated to cause disaffection'. This article was most likely a letter printed on 19 August which complained about the treatment of Volunteers imprisoned after the Rising. Also in Munster, Skibbereen's *Southern Star* was put out of circulation for a month in November 1916 after it criticised the Dublin Metropolitan Police (DMP).

It may well be that these incidents encouraged other newspapers to institute self-censorship and to keep within the limitations imposed by DORA. In 1917 there were only three suppressions: two Limerick-based labour papers, the *Factionist* and the *Irish Republic*, were permanently closed down, while the *Kilkenny People* was suppressed for three months. The paper's crime was to have been an open supporter of Sinn Féin candidates in that year's various by-elections. While Dublin Castle felt safe in closing regional newspapers, there was some official nervousness, at least in 1917, about enforcing such punishments on national newspapers, as can be seen in the case of the *Freeman's Journal*.

The death of Thomas Ashe in Mountjoy Jail in September 1917, after being force-fed while on hunger strike, caused immense anger across Ireland and much recrimination in

Left: The ruined premises of the *Freeman's Journal* on Prince's Street, beside the GPO in Dublin, which were destroyed by fire after the Easter Rising. (NLI)

Opposite page: Thomas Chapman, owner of the *Westmeath Independent*, and family. Under Chapman's ownership, the *Independent* became closely aligned with Sinn Féin by 1918. (Westmeath County Library Service)

the press. In an attempt to manage the public response, Decies warned the press not to publish speeches or letters that could cause 'disaffection', but his warning was ignored by the *Freeman's Journal*. The censor had given the press explicit instructions not to publish an open letter to newspapers from the bishop of Killaloe, Dr Michael Fogarty, in which he accused the British government of trampling over the rights of 'small nationalities'. The *Freeman* printed the letter and, despite much debate within Dublin Castle, went unpunished.

Yet 1918 would see the beginning of a prolonged period of confrontation between Irish newspapers and Dublin Castle. By 1918 many regional papers carried regular news items on local Sinn Féin political activities—after all, the increasingly successful and vibrant party was not a story they could afford to ignore. This emerging aspect of Irish newspapers was noted in Royal Irish Constabulary (RIC) reports from around the country, and its development was hastened by the conscription crisis in spring 1918.

Take, for example, the case of the *Westmeath Independent*, based in Athlone. The paper, owned by the Chapman family, had been allied with the Irish Parliamentary Party at the outbreak of the First World War, but under the editorship of Michael McDermott-Hayes had become an increasingly vocal supporter of Sinn Féin. The paper was suppressed for three weeks during April 1918 because of its vociferous opposition to conscription. The case was widely publicised by newspapers across the country, and Decies claimed that the suppression had 'an effect of the most salutary nature on the whole Irish press'. That was undoubtedly Decies's intention but the closure of the Athlone paper does not seem to have intimidated the Irish press. Indeed, on returning to news-stands, the *Westmeath Independent* maintained its previous editorial policy, and during that December's general election the paper was supportive of two local Sinn Féin candidates, Laurence Ginnell in Westmeath and

Harry Boland in South Roscommon.

The newspaper press, as a whole, was now more willing to confront Dublin Castle and to publish material that risked drawing official accusations of causing disaffection. The *Clare Champion*, the *Mayo News*, the *Tullamore & King's County Independent* and the Newcastle West *Weekly Observer* were also suppressed during March and April 1918 for their opposition to conscription and support of Sinn Féin. An instructive example is that of William Martin Murphy's *Irish Independent*. Murphy had publicly supported Irish recruitment to the British army earlier in the war but his paper was now a leading opponent of the government's decision to introduce conscription. The *Independent* asserted that 'Promise after promise to the Irish people has been broken by the Government, with the result that they have destroyed voluntary recruiting in this country'. The *Independent* offered an alternative to conscription: 'Grant the country full self-government', it advised, and then the British government 'could withdraw thousands of troops from Ireland for a theatre where they are

more needed, and would be more serviceable'. Almost every day over April and May 1918 the *Independent* warned that conscription would lead to disaster and, most likely, a widespread rebellion. Yet, as in the case of the *Freeman's Journal* in 1917, Dublin Castle proved unwilling to punish a national newspaper to the same extent as those in the regions.

British plans to impose conscription were ultimately abandoned in the face of widespread public hostility, and the Irish press reflected and reported that hostility. Over the remainder of 1918, Sinn Féin continued to grow in popularity and an increasingly nervous Dublin Castle responded by intensifying its censorship of Irish newspapers, especially after the arrival of Sir John French as lord lieutenant and Edward Shortt as chief secretary in May 1918 (the latter was subsequently replaced by Ian Macpherson in January 1919). Indeed, in Ireland, the DORA censorship regime remained in place even after the end of the war in November 1918. During the year, the *Ballina Herald*, the *Evening Herald*, the *Galway Express*, the *Meath Chronicle* and the *Southern Star* had all endured

EVENING HERALD

LADIES' COSTUMES AND BLOUSES
PRESCOTT'S DYE WORKS:

£1 TO £1,0
KELLY'S
GREAT CENTRAL MONEY
48 FLEET S

VOL. 26, NO. 235.   DUBLIN, MONDAY, OCTOBER 1, 1917.   ONE PENNY.

2 RAIDS ON LONDON

Ten Raiders Break Through the Defences

TWENTY PERSONS KILLED

KILLED	INJURED	TOTAL
872	2,216	3,088

30,000 MOURNERS

Incidents in Yesterday's Mighty Funeral

FACTS AND FIGURES

3 Miles of Marchers in Massed Formation

TO THOMAS ASHE.

In the majesty of Death we leave you sleeping, Thomas Ashe,
Gallant-hearted, brave and true,
You have fought a clean fight through.

And we, kneeling in the gloom
By the shadow of your tomb,
See the sun of Ireland rise
Brighter for your sacrifice.

In the majesty of Death we leave you sleeping, Thomas Ashe.

—Dorothy Hungerford (Mrs.).

Cramp! Cramp!! Cramp!!!

IN MOUNTJOY

Demands Granted to the Prisoners

MEN AT THE MATER

May Go Home During This Week

J.P.'S SUDDEN DEATH.

POUNDING AWAY

Artillery Active Along West Front

BRILLIANT ITALIAN SUCCE

From Sir Douglas Haig

From General Petain

---

periods of suppression. Those suppressions offered a hint of what was to come. In 1919 there would be nearly 30 separate newspaper suppressions, as the Castle made intensive, if futile, attempts to undermine Sinn Féin and the Dáil Éireann counter-state that emerged after the 1918 general election.

Sinn Féin emerged as an enormously successful political force in the years after the Easter Rising, as evidenced by its subsequent electoral successes. The attendant decline of the Irish Parliamentary Party caused much of the press to modify its attitude to Sinn Féin, partly because the papers sought to make themselves more amenable to the changing political affiliations of their readers. In addition, many newspapers became increasingly embittered by the actions of the British government during the remainder of the war, deploring the possibility of partition in any Irish political settlement, opposing conscription and attacking censorship. Indeed, shortly after the 1918 general election, the *Freeman's Journal* expressed an attitude shared by many newspapers: 'The Irish indictment of the censorship is not on the grounds that it keeps Englishmen in the dark, but that it denies to Irishmen elementary rights, which is the very badge of serfdom'. By that time, the relationship between Dublin Castle and the bulk of the Irish press was on the verge of collapse, with consequences that would become manifest during the later War of Independence.

Ian Kenneally is the editor of The Revolution Papers: 1923–1949.

Further reading

F. Larkin and M. O'Brien (eds), *Irish periodicals and journalism in twentieth-century Ireland* (Four Courts Press, 2014).

I. Kenneally, *The paper wall: newspapers and propaganda in Ireland, 1919–1921* (The Collins Press, 2008).

B. Novick, *Conceiving revolution* (Four Courts Press, 2001).

K. Rafter (ed.), *Irish journalism before independence* (Four Courts Press, 2011).

Above: The front cover of the *Evening Herald*, 1 October 1917. A report on the funeral of Thomas Ashe nestles between coverage of German air raids on London and fighting on the Western Front. (NLI)

The Irish Parliamentary Party in Great Britain, 1916–18.

HOME RULE, HOME FRONTS

BY **DARRAGH GANNON**

T. P. O'CONNOR, M.P.

PHOTO BY
ELLIOTT & FRY
LONDON.

'History is written by the victors', philosophised Walter Benjamin. Home Rule Ireland, by such definition, had its share of pyrrhic histories and historians during the First World War. Tom Kettle's *The ways of war* (1917), William O'Brien's *The downfall of parliamentarianism* (1918) and Stephen Gwynn's *John Redmond's last years* (1919) successively chronicled Home Rule's 'lost' victories in the climactic years of the Great War. The history of Home Rule, however, was being written, polemically and politically, across many home fronts. The Irish Parliamentary Party (IPP) in Great Britain, led by the storied Liverpool-Scotland MP T.P. O'Connor, experienced political transformation between 1916 and 1918 in collective British–Irish context. Writing the 'Irish in Great Britain' into the Home Rule history book *Irish heroes in the war* (1917), O'Connor established a resolute, representative and relevant 'British' IPP: 'such, then, are we, the Irish of Great Britain—united, unanimous, standing by the Allies with our hearts and with our brave children. That was our position at the beginning of the War; that is our position now. We are unchanged, we are unchangeable.' This essay interrogates that 'unchanging' narrative of the Irish Party in Great Britain between 1916 and 1918, and asks afresh how Irish Home Rule was lost on the British Home Front.

To many contemporary critics and historians, T.P. O'Connor was the 'English face' of the IPP. A regular contributor to current affairs in broadsheet newspapers (*Daily Telegraph*) and commentator on 'current affairs' in tabloids (*The Star, The Sun, M.A.P.*), O'Connor was the only IPP MP to be elected in a British constituency, standing successfully at Liverpool-Scotland between 1885 and 1929. He also presided over successive IPP organisations: the Irish National League of Great Britain

Left: T.P. O'Connor (1848–1929) was a Home Ruler and MP for Liverpool (Scotland) for almost 50 years. After the 1918 general election and the decimation of the Irish Parliamentary Party, he effectively stood as an independent until his death in 1929. (NLI)

T. P. O'CONNOR
went to America on an English Cruiser to collect funds for the Irish Party.

DR. PAT. McCARTAN
went to America, disguised as a stoker on a tramp steamer, to put the case for Irish Independence before the American Government. Which of these two is working for Ireland?

VOTE FOR
McCARTAN

Printed by P. MAHON, Dublin, and published by the Candidate.

(INLGB) and the United Irish League of Great Britain (UILGB). Between 1900 and 1914, membership of the UILGB increased from 8,000 to 47,000. Members were exhorted to subscribe to the Irish Parliamentary Fund, to propagate the virtues of Home Rule, and to vote Liberal in municipal and general elections. Indeed, within the UILGB Home Rule was framed as both an Irish and a British Question. Lecture topics ranged from Irish republican principles to British democracy; speakers included former Fenians and Liberal sympathisers, while members were mobilised on issues from Irish land reform to British legislative reform. At the height of the Ulster crisis (1913–14), John Redmond and other IPP MPs addressed Home Rule/ Liberal rallies in Birmingham, Cardiff, Glasgow and Manchester.

The First World War redirected efforts to the Home Front campaign. T.P. O'Connor now championed

● Above: Sinn Féin election poster highlighting the ways in which the IPP and Sinn Féin both plugged into American support for the Irish cause in different ways. (NLI)

enlistment in the British armed forces from public platforms. Meanwhile, *T.P.'s Journal of Great Deeds of the Great War*, begun in October 1914, serialised 'war enthusiasm' for the censored reader; he would later be awarded presidency of the British Board of Film Censors. By the spring of 1916 the Irish in Great Britain were reputed to have contributed 150,000 personnel to the British armed forces. Hollowed out by the success of voluntary enrolment, the UILGB maintained an organisation in outline. Its executive council circulated 'Irish Brigade' recruitment posters and ladies' branches hosted convalescing soldiers, while members discussed wartime issues such as the Derby Scheme. Nonetheless, neither the 1915 nor the 1916 UILGB convention took place.

To the IPP in Great Britain, the 1916 Rising was a First World War event. News of the 'Sinn Féin' rebellion and its 'gallant allies in Europe' coincided with recurrent Zeppelin raids over British centres. Unsurprisingly, therefore, the reactions of UILGB branches were of disapproval and dissociation: 'treacherous action', 'wickedness', 'insanity', 'horror', 'unpatriotic conduct'. Nevertheless, the detention of internees in British prisons thereafter mobilised a wartime humanitarian politics. Leading Home Rule figures in Glasgow, Liverpool and Manchester joined advanced nationalists on relief committees for the interned rebels, offering financial, material and moral support. Members of the London UILGB, however, were distanced from the advanced nationalist Irish National Relief Fund. IPP involvement in this campaign, in any case, had declined significantly by the autumn. The Home Front was replete with worthy charitable causes, such as the Prince of Wales National Relief Fund. The Somme, moreover, inflicted death and dependence directly on immigrant lives. The Tyneside Irish Brigade alone suffered over 1,100 casualties on 1 July. In the aftermath of the insurrection, meanwhile, T.P. O'Connor came to view Easter Week as merely 'incidental' in the context

of Home Rule legislative certainty.

It was to the Houses of Parliament that O'Connor attributed greatest political currency. He immersed himself in life at Westminster, shuttling between IPP sessions and meetings with Coalition ministers, while speaking on the future Irish administration from the benches. His belief in the virtues of parliament was absolute, his faith in British political leaders almost as complete. Indeed, despite the failure of the Lloyd George negotiations, F.S.L. Lyons judged him still 'hypnotized' by the 'Welsh wizard' as late as 1917. In contradistinction to other IPP leaders, O'Connor continued to frequent London's political 'clublands' in search of financial support for the Home Rule movement, an approach criticised by his Dublin-based colleague John Dillon: 'to a campaign amongst your English friends I do make a most emphatic objection. It won't do. The movement cannot be saved by such means. And if all is lost we had better go down decently.' O'Connor, ultimately, would tour America between June 1917 and August 1918 on behalf of the IPP, and, more contentiously, the Allied war effort.

The politics of war gradually strangled the Home Rule movement in Great Britain. While UILGB resolutions endorsing John Redmond and the IPP continued to be published in the *Weekly Freeman* in the early months of 1917, the lack of visits from party MPs to provincial branches was increasingly noted. Members, moreover, criticised the Coalition government's inaction over Home Rule legislation. Disillusioned, supporters cautioned against entertaining any 'extravagant hopes' for the Irish Convention. Nationalist frustrations were undoubtedly sharpened by wartime exigencies. This was the year of queue and shortage. In the wake of the German unrestricted submarine warfare campaign, British society was faced with increased food privations. The dearth of potatoes was a particular grievance within Irish communities, one Southampton trader being forced to advertise 'books exchanged for potatoes'. Irish nationalist complaints thus fed into a wider wartime mistrust of government authority.

Events in Ireland also undermined the IPP. Its 1917 by-election defeats by Sinn Féin were comprehensively analysed in the Irish Catholic press, the IPP consistently being presented as disorganised, weak and, above all, compromised by its dependence on the British Liberal Party. Sinn Féin clubs in London, Liverpool, Manchester and Glasgow, meanwhile, discretely emerged out of extant Rising relief committees, Gaelic League branches and IRB sections. The UILGB's response was indicative of underlying concern: 'there has never been a moment in the history of the organisation when there was greater need for its existence and for a determined resolve to strengthen it … the Irish in Great Britain are ready, resolute and united to accept a challenge from any quarter'.

That challenge proved to be the Irish conscription crisis. The passing of the Military Service Bill on 11 April 1918 caused outrage. UILGB branches published resolutions demanding a Home Rule parliament, while others proposed industrial action. The Irish in Great Britain, of course, had already crossed the conscription Rubicon; its application to Ireland, however, transgressed the rights of democracy, self-determination and small nations for which lives were being lost. Were British war aims an empty formula? Military compulsion in Ireland, further, contrasted sharply with political progress in Great Britain. The Representation of the People Act, which received the royal assent on 6 February, focused Home Rule minds on reconstruction. British branches, accordingly, discussed an expanded ethnic presence in parliament under proportional representation, the organisation of female voters and the emergence of the Labour Party as a significant political force.

T.P. O'Connor's return in August 1918, it was anticipated, would direct Home Rule organisation through these transformative British and Irish

IRISH NATIONAL RELIEF FUND.

OFFICES:—87, FULWOOD HOUSE, FULWOOD PLACE, HOLBORN, W.C.

OBJECTS.—To render assistance to the relatives and dependants of those who were executed, or otherwise lost their lives, or have been deported and imprisoned in connection with the Irish insurrection; and also to provide necessities in the way of food and clothing for those who are still imprisoned or interned in England.

AN APPEAL.

NO DOOM OF LAW condemns to privation and penalty the relatives of imprisoned men, or the families of the sentenced Dead. The voice of Justice forbids that injury shall be inflicted upon the innocent. God's precepts command us to comfort those who mourn, to assist those who are bereaven and to protect the fatherless child. Many are the mourners in Ireland to-day, many are the bereaven, many are the children fatherless, many are the homes made desolate.

We appeal for immediate and national aid on behalf of the destitute families of some 300 men slain during the insurrection, of 15 executed by Courts-Martial, of 158 condemned to penal servitude, of nearly 3,000 deported without trial. In all there have been between 3,000 and 4,000 cases of imprisonment : of these 1,619 are still interned and 158 imprisoned in England, the remainder having been released apparently because there was no charge against them ; but no compensation has been made for their wrongful imprisonment.

It adds to the urgency of the appeal that many of these have been deprived of their employment, and that some of the female relatives of accused men have, entirely distinct and without reproach, been heartlessly dismissed from their occupation, and despoiled of their livelihood.

Shall the voice of Justice, then, be unheard, and the Innocent be compelled to suffer injury, without sympathy and without redress ? Shall the dictates of Christianity be despised, which announce a blessing on the lovers of righteousness and declare that those only who show mercy shall obtain mercy on the great day of perfect Justice ?

We make our appeal to all human hearts, whose noble compassion can reach over every obstacle to redress wrongs and alleviate suffering, that they may co-operate in this merciful and righteous work. For the sake of our country we make it, of our Nation's honour, and of our own, so that its high repute for justice shall be transmitted by our generation unsullied to future and happier times.

Mrs. Clement Shorter.	Rev. Fr. W. W. Leonard.	Bro. O'Donnell.	Robert Lynd.
Miss Eva Gore-Booth.	„ „ R. Moore.	Dr. Alex. MacDonnell.	Owen Ward.
Mrs. Ginnell.	„ „ B. Murphy.	„ J. Reidy.	Luke Brady.
Mrs. Dryhurst.	„ Campbell.	„ Mark Ryan.	Jerh. O'Brien.
Mrs. Crilly.	„ „ J. M. Kearney.	„ O'Connell.	J. H. MacDonnell.
Mrs. Cavanagh.	„ „ F. Cassels.	„ Cotter.	J. C. Nolan.
Miss Nora Walsh.	„ „ O'Connor.	„ England, LL.D.	W. M. Harnett.
Miss Agnes MacHale.	„ „ P. H. Murray.	M. J. Fitzgerald.	M. J. Doherty.
Very Rev. Mgr. Canon W. F.	„ „ W. L. O'Farrell.	H. E. M. Bradley.	Richard Murray.
Brown, V.G.	„ „ Devine.	Wm. MacCarthy.	John J. McGrath.
Rev. Dr. J. Byrne O'Connell,	„ „ J. Thornton.	W. P. Ryan.	C. B. Dutton.
Ph.D.	„ „ J. Kelly.	Thos. Martin.	J. Cassidy.
Rev. Fr. T. O'Sullivan.	„ „ V. W. Magrath.	Edward Morrissey.	J. J. Fintan Murphy.
„ „ W. Kent, O.S.C.	Dr. M. Crowley.	Dr. Ml. Ryan.	Art O'Brien.

SUBSCRIPTIONS.—A sum of over £350 has already been received as a result of private collection. Whilst donations will be very gratefully received the committee wish to point out the probability of the need for Relief being of long duration, and in the circumstances they are very anxious to obtain promises of regular weekly or monthly contributions.

DISTRIBUTION.—A considerable portion of the money already collected has been spent in supplying necessities of food and clothing to prisoners in Wandsworth, Woking, Lewes, Stafford, Knutsford, Wakefield, &c., and other amounts have already been sent to the Irish National Aid Association, and the Irish Volunteer Dependants Fund in Dublin.

Cheques and other remittances should be made payable to "THE IRISH NATIONAL RELIEF FUND" and crossed "London & Provincial Bank, Holborn Branch," and all communications addressed to the Fund at address given above.

COMMITTEE OF MANAGEMENT.

Chairman.—RICHARD MURRAY.   Vice-Chairman.—JOHN J. McGRATH
Hon. Treasurers.—C. B. DUTTON, JOSEPH CASSIDY.   Hon. Secretaries.—ART O'BRIEN, J. J. FINTAN MURPHY.

Any further information or particulars will be most gladly given to anyone interested.

" Catholic Times " Office, Liverpool.

politics. This proved illusory. The UILGB's October convention, attended by O'Connor, John Dillon and Joseph Devlin, demonstrated the distance between the party leadership and members in British centres. Delegates from 141 branches called for a repudiation of the perceived IPP–Liberal alliance in favour of a formal relationship with Labour. Dillon's statement that 'we are no more in alliance with the Liberal Party than we are in alliance with the German Emperor' did not convince. Nor did the party's recent record in Ireland. The UILGB's annual report estimated membership income to have reached only £1,544 14s 7d, its lowest figure in twenty years. This sharp decline in support was accounted for by the 'blunders and falsified promises of the Government' and the 'spread of a

●

Above: Irish National Relief Fund poster published in Liverpool and seeking financial support to aid Irish prisoners in English internment camps c. 1916. (NLI)

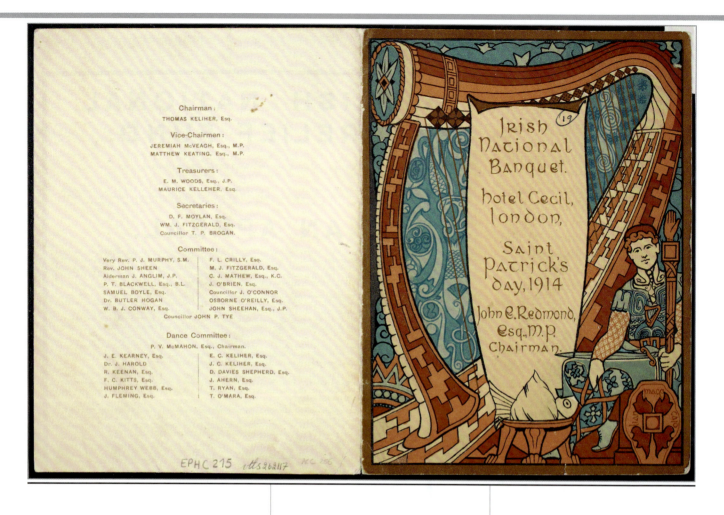

Chairman:
THOMAS KELIHER, Esq.

Vice-Chairmen:
JEREMIAH McVEAGH, Esq., M.P.
MATTHEW KEATING, Esq., M.P.

Treasurers:
E. M. WOODS, Esq., J.P.
MAURICE KELLEHER, Esq.

Secretaries:
D. F. MOYLAN, Esq.
WM. J. FITZGERALD, Esq.
Councillor T. P. BROGAN.

Committee:

Very Rev. P. J. MURPHY, S.M. | F. L. CRILLY, Esq.
Rev. JOHN SHEEN | M. J. FITZGERALD, Esq.
Alderman J. ANGLIM, J.P. | C. J. MATHEW, Esq., K.C.
P. T. BLACKWELL, Esq., B.L. | J. O'BRIEN, Esq.
SAMUEL BOYLE, Esq. | Councillor J. O'CONNOR
Dr. BUTLER HOGAN | OSBORNE O'REILLY, Esq.
W. B. J. CONWAY, Esq. | JOHN SHEEHAN, Esq., J.P.
Councillor JOHN P. TYE

Dance Committee:
P. V. McMAHON, Esq., Chairman.

J. E. KEARNEY, Esq. | E. C. KELIHER, Esq.
Dr. J. HAROLD | J. C. KELIHER, Esq.
R. KEENAN, Esq. | D. DAVIES SHEPHERD, Esq.
F. C. KITTS, Esq. | J. AHERN, Esq.
HUMPHREY WEBB, Esq. | T. RYAN, Esq.
J. FLEMING, Esq. | T. O'MARA, Esq.

Irish National Banquet.
hotel Cecil, london,
Saint Patrick's Day, 1914
John E. Redmond, Esq., M.P. Chairman.

doctrine impracticable in its ends and foolish in its means'.

The December 1918 general election reinforced the IPP's wartime decline. Canvassing London constituencies, T.P. O'Connor noted the dissolution of support: 'there is great unrest among our branches … our people will go wholesale into the Labour movement and desert our movement'. Irish Labour parties, further, would later emerge in South Wales and on Tyneside. Sinn Féin also emerged, finally, as a political alternative to the IPP. Between January and March 1919, republican-inspired demonstrations were held in London, Liverpool, Manchester and Glasgow in solidarity with the imprisoned 'German plot' detainees. Speakers addressed crowds of up to 5,000 people through that essential post-war discourse: self-determination. The platform politics of the 'Sinn Féin celebrities', T.P. O'Connor observed from a distance, 'may arrest the attention of a hurried world

better than our old-world rational methods'. By April Sinn Féin had established the Irish Self-Determination League of Great Britain. Although public debates over the future of the Home Rule movement continued into the summer, membership outside Lancashire and Scotland fell dramatically. By September 1919 only three UILGB branches remained in London.

Although entertaining fantasies of declaring the IPP in Great Britain in favour of 'self-determination' and taking over the Irish Self-Determination League from the inside, O'Connor was resigned in reality to the role of isolated parliamentary observer, neatly denoted by his title: 'father of the House of Commons'. He would continue to serve the Home Rule movement at Westminster, one of only eight remaining IPP MPs. It was pyrrhic history, thus, that the Government of Ireland Bill was written into the statute books in October 1919. Irish

Home Rule was lost on the British Home Front.

Darragh Gannon is a Research Fellow in the School of History, Anthropology, Philosophy and Politics at Queen's University, Belfast.

Further reading

L.W. Brady, *T.P. O'Connor and the Liverpool-Irish* (London, 1983).

D. MacRaild, *The Irish diaspora in Britain, 1750–1939* (Basingstoke, 2011).

T.P. O'Connor, *Memoirs of an old parliamentarian* (London, 1929).

A. O'Day, 'Irish diaspora politics in perspective: the United Irish Leagues of Great Britain and America in perspective, 1900–14', in D. MacRaild (ed.), *The Great Famine and beyond: Irish migrants in Britain in the nineteenth and twentieth centuries* (Dublin, 2000).

●

Above: A decorative invitation to the Irish National Banquet being held in the Hotel Cecil in London on St Patrick's Day, 1914. (NLI)

'The Irish question will not be settled by the recognition of Irish nationality: it will be let loose by it for the first time'
(Bernard Shaw to the chairman of the Irish Convention, 3 August 1917).

BERNARD SHAW AND THE 1917 IRISH CONVENTION

BY **PETER GAHAN**

On Monday morning, 15 April 1918, a world-famous Irish writer trudged over two miles through a rainstorm from his home in the English village of Ayot St Lawrence, Hertfordshire, to nearby Wheathampstead to buy a newspaper. Bernard Shaw needed to know whether the *Manchester Guardian* had published a letter of his, a last-ditch effort to provoke the British government to implement 'some form of Irish Home Rule *before* the end of the Great War. Shaw's letter was printed, along with an approving editorial, yet proved futile in forestalling years of violence in Ireland to achieve practically the same end.

Shaw had spent the previous year actively involved with the Irish Convention convened by Prime Minister Lloyd George in June 1917. Chaired by his friend Horace Plunkett, the Convention would let Irishmen decide how Home Rule should be implemented following the 1916 Easter Rising. History, however, wrecked Shaw's and Plunkett's—and Ireland's—hopes when, as the Convention finished its deliberations, the German army under General Ludendorff launched a massive attack on British lines, five offensives in two

Below: The Irish Convention in session at Trinity College Dublin's Regent House, based on a painting by Walter Paget. (NLI)

The Irish Convention 1917-18
In full session at Trinity College Dublin

weeks, panicking the British government. The British Army alone lost around 300,000 men, with the 36th (Ulster) Division and the 16th (Irish) Division among the hardest hit. Plunkett, then in London, wrote (29 March 1918) that 'the biggest battle in the world's history—the biggest by far—is raging only 2 to 3 hours away from here by aeroplane!' In Dublin a week later, wrapping up the Convention's Irish secretariat's work, Plunkett wrote to Shaw (8 April 1918): 'My dear G.B.S., I am crossing over [to London] to-night, the bearer of the Irish Convention's Report. I do not know how many days I shall be in town but we must meet and have a talk over what is to be done next.' Next day, Plunkett delivered the

report to the government, and then watched in horror as Lloyd George in the House of Commons introduced military conscription to Ireland (previously exempt), shattering in a single stroke any hope held out by the Convention's recommendation of a peaceful transition to Home Rule for the whole island: 'As devoid of military advantage as it was fraught with political disaster', lamented Plunkett. After discussing the resultant full-scale Irish political crisis with Plunkett two days later, Shaw wrote his letter to the *Manchester Guardian*, and that weekend Shaw and his wife Charlotte, an even more determined Irish nationalist than her husband, met also with Stephen Gwynn MP, who had led the Irish Parliamentary

Party Convention delegates after John Redmond's death.

Shaw first became involved with the Convention ten months earlier, when Plunkett's colleague, the poet, artist, journal editor and agricultural organiser George Russell, known as Æ, published his 'Thoughts for a Convention' in the *Irish Times*. Shaw responded privately to Æ, whom he knew personally, differing only on one significant—for Shaw—point. Shaw wanted to propose a 'supranational' context for an independent Ireland with its immediate neighbours to supersede the United Kingdom of Great Britain and Ireland: a federation of four co-equal nations (Ireland, England, Scotland and Wales) on the two islands. Æ sent Shaw's letter on to the *Irish Times* (1 June 1917), marking the beginning of his most sustained engagement with Irish constitutional politics.

With encouragement from Plunkett, Shaw hoped to be appointed a delegate to the Convention, either by the prime minister like Æ (appointed to keep lines of communication open with Sinn Féin, who were sure to boycott the Convention) or by the Irish political parties, or even by the Convention itself (unlikely, given Shaw's tendency to controversy). When Shaw's Irish Fabian friend Lion Phillimore (born Lucy Fitzpatrick) noted the total absence of women delegates, Shaw suggested (18 July 1917) that an alternative, 'unofficial convention [be held] by the women, consisting of *men and women*, by way of protest, if I thought the requisite public talent would be forthcoming, or that anyone but the Countess Markievicz would take it up'. As bad for Shaw was the delegates' attempt at their first meeting in Trinity College, Dublin, to appoint an Englishman as chairman (30 July 1917): 'How they could have perpetrated such an insensate *gaffe* as to even propose Hopwood … an Englishman, without a single tie to Ireland … [W]as it the Irish instinct to trust anybody rather than an Irishman?'

Shaw's ultimate failure to secure

a nomination, however, left him free to voice his own proposals openly, and Plunkett kept Shaw fully informed of the Convention's proceedings by using him to vet the chairman's secret report to the king, which Plunkett sent on to Shaw in instalments. Thus Plunkett and Shaw remained in constant written contact during the Convention's proceedings, and on his frequent visits over to the Convention secretariat in London Plunkett would meet with the Shaws, while for ten days in October 1917 they stayed at Plunkett's house,

● Above: Shaw was a vocal commentator on public affairs; he is pictured here at an anti-vivisection rally in London's Trafalgar Square, *c.* 1910. (*HI* 24.1)

● Opposite page: George Russell (Æ): his 'Thoughts for a convention', published in the *Irish Times* in early 1917, prompted Shaw's engagement with the embryonic Irish Convention. (NGI)

Kilteragh, in Foxrock, Co. Dublin, to discuss Convention matters with Plunkett, Æ and members of the Convention's Irish secretariat like Frank Cruise O'Brien and Erskine Childers. Plunkett operated Kilteragh, which Shaw likened to a Picasso painting, like a national cultural centre where people of all political hues with an interest in Ireland's future could gather.

At Plunkett's request, Shaw wrote a quasi-formal letter to the chairman setting out what the Convention should do and the solutions it might propose. Dismissing the succession of Home Rule bills, Shaw was sceptical also of written constitutions (3 August 1917):

'We must be a free nation: that is, we must govern ourselves according to our own ideas and interests in our own way; and our constitution must grow out of such gov-

ernment and be a live, growing, changing body of thought and custom, and not a written document giving us leave to do this and forbidding us to do that and making the other *ultra vires* for us … A parliament is a constitution in itself: if it is limited it is not a parliament.'

Shaw also pushed his federal solution before concluding:

'The Irish question will not be settled by the recognition of Irish nationality: it will be let loose by it for the first time.'

In Kerry that summer, Shaw studied the history of the constitutional conventions and legislation that set up Australia, Canada and South Africa as independent constitutional entities within the Empire. All were federations, as was Britain's

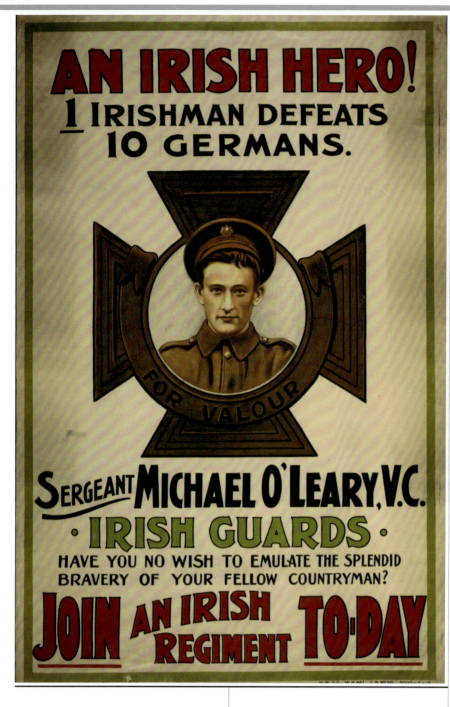

AN IRISH HERO!
1 IRISHMAN DEFEATS
10 GERMANS.

FOR VALOUR

SERGEANT MICHAEL O'LEARY, V.C.
• IRISH GUARDS •
HAVE YOU NO WISH TO EMULATE THE SPLENDID
BRAVERY OF YOUR FELLOW COUNTRYMAN?

JOIN AN IRISH REGIMENT TO-DAY

Above: A recruiting poster depicting Irish Victoria Cross-winner Michael O'Leary, who was widely assumed to be the model for Shaw's comic one-act play *O'Flaherty VC* (an assumption denied by Shaw). The play marked Shaw's earliest engagement with Irish politics in the revolutionary period but was withdrawn prior to its opening run at the Abbey Theatre in 1915 owing to British concerns that it would discourage recruitment. (Library of Congress)

most important former colony, the United States, reinforcing his conviction that federation could be key also for Ireland. Plunkett's own preference was dominion status for Ireland, like Canada's, but Shaw was sceptical, considering Ireland as geographically too close—unlike Canada—to prevent British political interference. Nevertheless, as chairman Plunkett wanted as many proposals debated inside the Convention as possible, so southern unionist Lord Dunraven would eventually submit a federal scheme along Shaw's lines.

With the Convention keeping the Irish Question in the news, an unexpected source, the unionist anti-socialist *Daily Express*, invited Shaw to detail his proposed solution in print. Shaw's three long articles were published simultaneously in London, New York, Belfast and Cork in late 1917, with his native Dublin settling for extracts only! The Talbot Press quickly issued them as a single pamphlet, *How to settle the Irish Question*.

Apart from his federal proposal that would transpose the Irish question to a two-islands/four-nations context, the articles critiqued both the Ulster unionists (anti-Home Rule in any form) and Sinn Féin, the latter having merged with the republican Irish Volunteers and replaced Arthur Griffith with Éamon de Valera as leader. Shaw wrote as the reconstituted Sinn Féin held its first national conference in October 1917—the 'opposition Convention', Plunkett called it. Shaw also attempted to diffuse, at Plunkett's request, the biggest issue dividing the Convention, fiscal union (as insisted on by unionists) or fiscal autonomy (as advocated by nationalists). Shaw felt that this should not be a question of doctrinaire *national* difference, while suggesting that an independent Ireland could gain as part of a larger economic grouping with Britain.

Surprisingly to some, particularly xenophobic nationalists, Shaw's rhetoric was almost stridently anti-English, evident also in his infamous anti-militarist *Common sense about the War*, written from the point of view of a neutral, objective Irish observer, which landed him in trouble in 1914. Shaw, though, was never anything other than rhetorically anti-English. Even as a convinced, if sometimes reluctant, Irish nationalist, he would retain some links with Britain: 'London and Dublin must always be stations on the same circulatory system. Geography and common sense make a political unit of the two islands. Nevertheless, we are a distinct nation.' His 1907 preface to *John Bull's other island* had first articulated the argument for Ireland's right to national independence as a natural right, language that—significantly—was taken up by Éamon de Valera during the Treaty negotiations.

Also in that preface, Shaw launched a scathing anti-colonial attack on Britain's administration of Egypt, which seemed curious, as not long before, to the disgust of British Liberals (and some Irish nationalists), he had defended the Empire against the Boers. Shaw, though, did not so much justify the Empire (an indefensible term, he thought) as prefer a British colonial administration, however bad, to the Afrikaners' seventeenth-century Calvinism that would later mutate into South Africa's apartheid regimes. As an anti-colonial internationalist—or imperialist, *faute de mieux*—Shaw had become increasingly impatient with Dublin Castle's inept handling of the Dublin Lockout of 1913, the Curragh Mutiny of 1914, the censorship of his play *O'Flaherty V.C.* in 1915, and the execution of Casement and the leaders of the Easter Rising in 1916; he thought that his public opposition to those executions might lend his voice weight during the Convention.

Another paradoxical constant for Shaw, whether speaking of dominion status for Ireland, Home Rule, federation, devolution during the treaty negotiations or, indeed, international relations in general, was that power must be conferred from the periphery to the centre, not devolved from the centre to the periphery. Britain, therefore, cannot grant Ireland powers to which it can already lay claim by natural right, whereas an independent Ireland could freely assign some sovereign power to a federation within the two islands—or, as would happen, to a European Union. Shaw's federal proposal could only occur if the four nations came together as independent co-equal states freely choosing such an agreement, with national independence having priority. Constantly trying to square the circle, he hoped that with the right public information campaign at the end of the war the two-step process might happen simultaneously.

On other issues like policing Shaw was prescient, criticising the final Convention report, which because of the war would leave control of the police with London:

'The explanation is worse than the offence; this is not the moment to remind our Bolsheviks and Dervishes [i.e. Nationalists and Unionists] that the R.I.C. is not really a police force, but a military occupation of a conquered country. Besides, it is not really true: they are so much an ordinary police force and nothing else … Leaving them under English control takes all the reality out of Home Rule in the most offensive possible way.'

The mostly Irish members of the two police forces soon became prime targets for nationalists in the Irish War of Independence.

In the end, the major unintended consequence of Lloyd George's linking of Irish military conscription to 32-county Home Rule was to unify all shades of Irish nationalism for the first time. The lord mayor of Dublin convened a meeting of all nationalist parties in the Mansion House on 18 April, a pledge-signing took place throughout Ireland on 21 April and, almost exactly two years after the Easter Rising, a resurgent labour movement organised the largest one-day general strike in Irish history on 23 April. This focusing of nationalist energies changed the direction of modern Irish history, making possible the huge political success of Sinn Féin in the December general election.

Staying in Kerry again in summer 1918, Shaw wrote *War issues for Irishmen*, still trying to make the British see sense on conscription. Although printed by Maunsels in Dublin, the pamphlet was withdrawn: Irish conscription, so urgent for the British in spring, proved unnecessary with the end of the war in sight but would leave a trail of wreckage in its wake in Ireland, as Plunkett, Æ and Shaw all feared. Æ explained it best to Lloyd George when resigning from the Convention (5 February 1918):

'We have for the first time in Ireland a disinterested nationalism not deriving its power from grievances connected with land or even

oppressive Government but solely from the growing self-consciousness of nationality, and this has with the younger generation all the force of a religion, with the carelessness about death, suffering or material loss which we find among the devotees of a religion. Any Government established which does not allow this national impulse free play, will be wrecked by it.'

Ignited by Lloyd George's Irish conscription *démarche* of April 1918, Ireland would soon follow the example of the United States' revolutionary war of independence, and the violence, which Shaw's letter to the *Manchester Guardian* had hoped to forestall, would begin.

Peter Gahan is co-editor of Palgrave Macmillan's Bernard Shaw and his Contemporaries *series.*

Further reading

T. Hennessey, *Dividing Ireland: World War I and Partition* (Oxford, 1998).

A. O'Day, *Irish Home Rule 1862–1921* (Manchester, 1998).

T. West, *Horace Plunkett, co-operation and politics: an Irish biography* (Gerrards Cross, 1986).

●

Above: George Bernard Shaw, pictured in 1914. (Library of Congress)

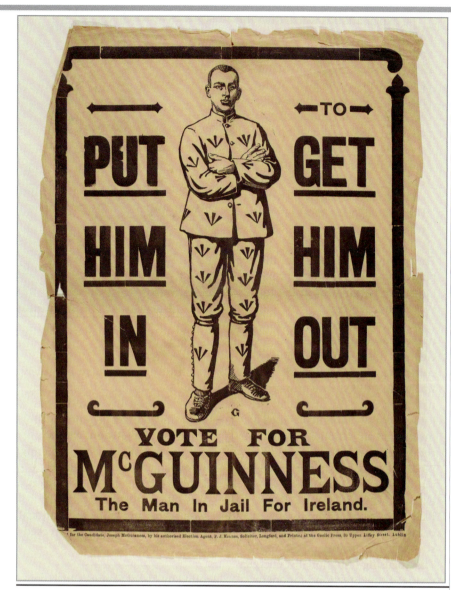

PUT HIM IN — TO — GET HIM OUT

VOTE FOR McGUINNESS
The Man In Jail For Ireland.

An analysis of the 1918 general election.

ANATOMY OF AN ELECTORAL LANDSLIDE

BY **BRIAN HANLEY**

On 14 December 1918 the election that changed Ireland forever took place. The Irish Parliamentary Party (IPP or Home Rule party), the dominant force in Irish nationalism for over a generation, was swept away in a landslide for Sinn Féin. The party that under John Redmond had thought itself on the verge of finally winning self-government was now reduced to just six out of 105 Irish seats. Sinn Féin, until 1916 a relatively marginal formation, which campaigned on the basis of refusing to attend parliament at Westminster at all, won 73 seats. Even more dramatically, that party, led by Éamon de Valera, was now formally republican, demanding independence from Britain and pledging to use 'any and every means available to render impotent the power of England to hold Ireland in subjection by military force or otherwise'. Though open to interpretation, this promise nevertheless offered a real challenge to the British authorities. A substantial minority of Irish opinion expressed a desire to maintain the constitutional *status quo*, however; Unionists won 26 seats, almost all of them in north-east Ulster.

There had not been a general election in the United Kingdom since 1910, and the interim had seen the carnage of the Great War, the Easter Rising, the election of four separatist candidates in 1917, the massive resistance to conscription in early 1918 and a government clampdown in May that year (the 'German plot') which further radicalised large sections of the population. All these factors could have produced upsets at the polls, but the widening of the franchise made a transformation much more likely. The Representation of the People Act (1918) effected the greatest single extension of the right to vote in Irish history. The proportion of the adult population eligible to vote jumped from 26.9% to 73.7%—from perhaps 698,000 voters to 1.93 million. The new legislation ended the 'head of household' register by abolishing property qualifications for men aged 21 or over, while enfranchising women over 30 who met minimum property qualifications as householders or the wives of householders. A whole swath of working-class and lower middle-class men, and some (usually better-off) women, had the vote for the first time. Perhaps just 360,000 of those who voted in 1918 had done so before. It was the first general election held on a single day and was fought under the 'first past the post' system, where the candidate who topped the poll took the seat. It was possible for an individual to contest several seats (de Valera stood in four and was elected for two constituencies). A further complicating factor in Ireland was that in 1910 two thirds of Home Rule MPs had been returned uncontested. Many areas had not actually seen an election since the 1890s. As a result of this, the IPP lacked organisation in much of the country. This contributed to its decision not to fight 24 constituencies at all. Therefore much of Munster (including County Cork, Kerry, parts of Limerick, Clare and Tipperary) and portions of Connacht and the midlands (some 475,000 voters) saw no contest at all.

In total, Sinn Féin polled 474,859 votes (46.9%), the Unionists polled 289,025 (28.5%) while the IPP took 220,226 (21.7%). These totals underestimate nationalist support, however, as both Sinn Féin and the IPP would have polled higher had there been elections in the uncontested constituencies (Unionists were unlikely to have stood in any of them). In fact, Sinn Féin would probably have won all of these seats. The uncontested County Cork constituencies, for example, had been lost in 1910 to the IPP's nationalist rival, the All For Ireland League (AFIL). Large sections of the AFIL had gone over to Sinn Féin by 1918. In the election itself, of the 37 constituencies where the IPP and Sinn Féin went head to head the republicans won on 35 occasions. An indication of the extraordinary nature of the poll was that many successful Sinn Féin candidates were not local and were not well known, and some were not even in Ireland during the campaign. Thirty-six of the candidates were in jail, six on the run from

the authorities and four in the United States. This reflected the harassment the Sinn Féin campaign faced from the state, with meetings broken up and canvassers arrested, as well as censorship of their election material. Despite this, in many areas Sinn Féin won stunning victories. In Cork city they polled over 20,000 votes to the IPP's 7,300. In Dublin city and county Sinn Féin took ten of the eleven seats, outpolling their Home Rule rivals by 79,400 votes to 36,638. In Galway South Sinn Féin's Frank Fahy took 10,621 votes; William Duffy of the IPP polled only 1,744. In Leitrim Sinn Féin won 17,711 votes, their rivals just 3,096. In Queen's County Sinn Féin's Kevin O'Higgins received 13,452 votes, well ahead of

the IPP's 6,480. The IPP leader, John Dillon, was defeated by de Valera in Mayo East by 8,975 votes to 4,514.

Other areas were more tightly contested, however. In Louth Sinn Féin's J.J. O'Kelly only defeated the Home Ruler Richard Hazelton by 255 votes. In Wexford Easter Rising veteran James Ryan faced a tough battle in a county with strong Redmondite traditions. In this case Ryan's work as a doctor locally during the influenza crisis helped him, and he defeated Peter ffrench of the IPP by 8,729 votes to 8,211. For the IPP to have any chance, they had to rely on every advantage their candidates might possess. Despite his family name, and strong popular support in areas such as Ballybricken, Captain

●

Right: A map of the 1918 general election results published by the Friends of Irish Freedom for distribution in America. (NLI)

●

Opposite page: Election poster of Joseph McGuinness, when he won the South Longford by-election for Sinn Féin in May 1917 while in jail. He was re-elected in the general election of December 1918. (UCD)

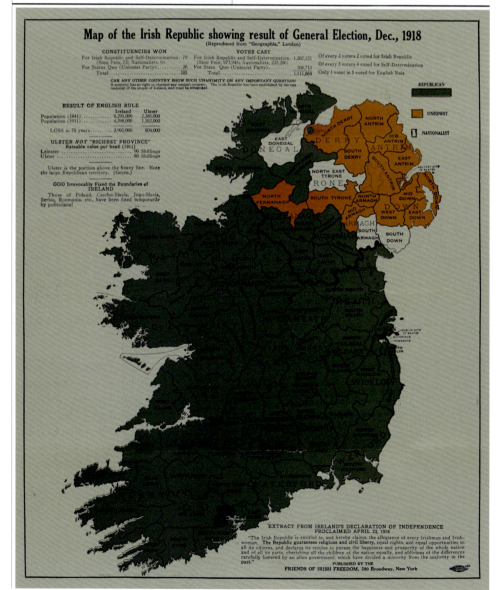

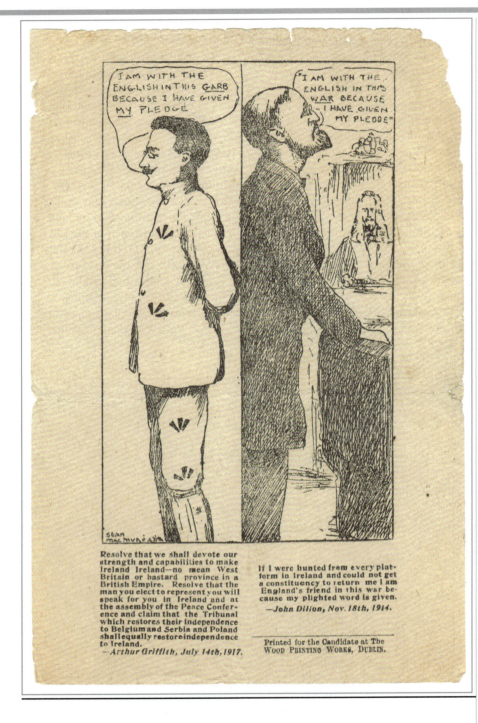

de Valera, nominally the Sinn Féin candidate, received just 33 votes. Though it won no seats in the city, Sinn Féin contested all nine Belfast constituencies, including Shankill (where they received 534 votes). The party took seats in Fermanagh South, North-West Tyrone and Derry City, however, as well as seats in Cavan, Monaghan and three of the Donegal constituencies.

Though their greatest successes came in Ulster, where they took 23 out of 38 seats, Unionists contested several constituencies in what later became the Free State. They polled respectably in Monaghan North (4,497) and Donegal East (4,797). In Cork city Unionists won 2,386 votes, in Wicklow West 2,600 and in the four Dublin constituencies 18,647 votes overall. Unionists also held the two Trinity College seats (elected on a restricted franchise), but the real surprise was Sir Maurice Dockrell's win in Rathmines, where he received more votes (7,400) than Sinn Féin and the IPP combined.

The Irish Volunteers played a major role in the election, coming from across Ireland (particularly Munster, where there were few elections to fight) to support Sinn Féin. They stewarded rallies, canvassed and protected polling booths. Their presence was needed, because in many areas the IPP literally went down fighting. Sinn Féin candidates were attacked and their premises wrecked, and running battles took place between rival supporters. In Ulster the IPP could call on the support of the Ancient Order of Hibernians. In many southern towns republicans claimed that ex-servicemen and their families, especially the 'Separation Women', were behind the attacks on them. Republicans tended to have a low opinion of their rivals. One claimed that in Waterford, during 1918, 'drink was flowing … to see that fanatical, separation-money mob, one could not help thinking what Daniel O'Connell thought when he said: "You should know the animals I was supposed to make a nation out of".' How much these impressions were influenced by class and gender bias is difficult to discern.

William Redmond only narrowly held his Waterford seat, beating Dr V.J. White of Sinn Féin by 4,915 votes to 4,431. The exception to the general pattern was in Ulster. Unionists won the majority of seats there, but the IPP also polled much better than elsewhere. Sharp inter-communal rivalries meant that the party was in better shape for the fight. Its greatest success came with Joseph Devlin's defeat of de Valera by 8,488 votes to 3,245 in Belfast's Falls constituency. The other four Ulster seats that the party took were uncontested by Sinn Féin, however. In the run-up to the election Cardinal Logue had obtained an agreement between the rival nationalist parties not to split their votes and allow Unionists to take extra seats. As a result (though their candidates' names appeared on the ballot paper), the IPP and Sinn Féin gave each other free runs in eight seats. Hence in South Down the IPP's Jeremiah McVeagh defeated the Unionist candidate by 8,756 votes to 5,573, while

Certainly much of the IPP's remaining support was driven by local loyalties, and it is clear that some of the urban poor remained loyal to the party. Nevertheless, Sinn Féin also benefited from its association with labour, the general strike against conscription and the revolutionary mood in post-war Europe. A number of union leaders spoke at Sinn Féin rallies. The party's election material appealed to workers to 'Keep Connolly's Flag Flying' and claimed that the demand for an Irish republic had 'the support of the Government of the Russian Republics and of the workers of France, Germany (and) Australia'. Certainly the decision of the Labour and Trade Union Congress not to stand candidates (despite an offer of a pact from Sinn Féin) gave republicans another advantage in its battle with the IPP. In Belfast, however, four candidates from the Labour Representation Committee did stand, winning 12,164 votes but no seats. Their best result was 3,674 for trade unionist Sam Kyle in Shankill, where he was well behind Labour Unionist Samuel McGuffin's 11,840.

While this was the first general election in which some women could vote, only Sinn Féin stood female candidates. Countess Markievicz was elected in Dublin's St Patrick's constituency, while Winifred Carney took just 539 votes in the largely Protestant Victoria constituency in Belfast. But 36% of the new electorate was female and one Dublin Unionist claimed that 'this was, to a great extent, a women's election'. Republican women had experience of political campaigning and were prominent in Sinn Féin's efforts. The Unionists also had a network of female activists who had cut their teeth during the Home Rule crisis, or in some cases in early suffrage campaigning. In contrast, the IPP may have suffered from its long-time hostility to, and neglect of, women's causes. Women, however, were also prominent among the urban crowds that clashed with republicans, though many of these, ironically, probably could not vote. As was usual in Irish elections, there were numerous allegations of skulduggery. Many republican activists accepted that their work involved 'personating … voting not only for dead people but for living ones who were known to be hostile'. In Cork it was alleged that the IPP personated in the morning and republicans in the afternoon and that this was seen by the public as a 'good joke'. Nevertheless, the scale of Sinn Féin's victory was only possible with genuine popular support.

The world war had ended with the promise of self-determination for nations, while revolutions in Russia and in Germany seemed to signal the collapse of the old imperialisms. All these factors contributed to Sinn Féin's triumph, but the republican movement was diverse. Sinn Féin candidates included many IRB members and Rising veterans, including Richard Mulcahy, Michael Collins and Harry Boland. Despite his countermanding order in 1916, Eoin MacNeill won two seats for the party. Arthur Griffith also took two seats and several candidates were supporters of his 'original' Sinn Féin. The party also attracted ex-Home Rulers. Sinn Féin director of elections, the businessman James O'Mara, was former IPP MP for Kilkenny South; in 1918 he became Sinn Féin TD for the same constituency. Sinn Féin's victory illustrated the popularity of the demand for self-determination; how that was to be achieved was still unclear. Despite the temptation to read events backwards, it was by no means obvious in 1918 what might happen next. The majority of voters rejected continued citizenship within the United Kingdom and thousands embraced the slogan of 'the Republic.'

Brian Hanley is an Irish History Research Fellow at the University of Edinburgh.

Further reading

J. Borgonovo, *The dynamics of war and revolution, Cork city 1916–1918* (Cork, 2013).

M. Laffan, *The resurrection of Ireland: the Sinn Féin Party 1916–1923* (Cambridge, 1999).

S. Paseta, *Irish nationalist women, 1900–1918* (Cambridge, 2016).

P. Yeates, *A city in wartime: Dublin 1914–1918* (Dublin, 2011).

● Above: A handbill invoking a series of historical events and figures in support of the Sinn Féin election campaign in 1918. (NLI)

● Opposite page: Leaflet issued in support of Arthur Griffith's candidature for the East Cavan parliamentary seat, 1918. (Kilmainham Gaol Museum)

SINN FEIN		THE OTHERS	
WE VOTED FOR INDEPENDENCE		WE DID NOT	
Brian Boru	1014	Dermot McMurrough (Traitor)	1168
Feagh McHugh O'Byrne	1596	King Henry II. of England	1172
Hugh Roe O'Donnell	1590	Queen Elizabeth of England	1590
Patrick Sarsfield	1691	Oliver Cromwell	1649
Wolfe Tone	1798	King William of Orange	1690
Edward Fitzgerald	1798	Major Sirr	1798
Michael Dwyer	1799	General Lake	1799
Joseph Holt	1800	Reynolds the Spy	1798
Robert Emmet	1803	Armstrong the Spy	1798
John Mitchel	1844	Bloody Balfour	1886
James Stephens	1867	Richard Pigott	1889
C. S. Parnell	1886	Edward Carson	1914
Patrick Pearse	1916	General Maxwell	1916
James Connolly	1916	Major Price	Still
Roger Casement	1916	Lord French	with us

WHICH SIDE WILL YOU VOTE?

EPILOGUE

This poem was originally published in the Dublin satirical magazine *Irish Fun* in April 1918, during the conscription crisis. While it makes no mention of Easter 1916, it takes a swipe at many of the luminaries of the Home Rule movement: John Redmond himself ('Honest John'), the influential veteran MP for Liverpool T.P. O'Connor ('Tay Pay', whose knack for fund-raising in the US was also referenced here), and the diminutive West Belfast MP Joe Devlin (the 'Mighty Atom') and his links to the Ancient Order of Hibernians. It strikes a sarcastic note in relation to the ongoing promise of Home Rule (the 'No Far Distant Date') and, obviously, Redmondite support for the war effort. It is tempting to think that the 'House that Jack built' refers to the version of Westminster that they presented to the Irish electorate, in which they retained sufficient influence to deliver Home Rule; if that is the case, the caustic final stanza points towards their perceived political failure, and their actual political defeat as Irish nationalist politics underwent a profound shift in allegiance. The house that Jack built fell down in December 1918.

JOHN GIBNEY

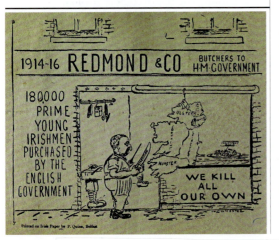

'The house that Jack built'

Tomás Ó hAmhlaidh

This is the House that Jack built,
This is the Party that fought and
    won,
And spoke and denounced the
    savage Hun,
To the great amusement of *Irish Fun*,
On the 'flure' of the House that
    Jack built.

This is the orator, Tay Pay,
Who went to beg money beyond
    the say,
And who holds an undisputed sway
Over the Party that fought and won,
And spoke and denounced the
    savage Hun,
To the great amusement of *Irish Fun*,
On the 'flure' of the House that
    Jack built.

This is the great and peerless one
Whom men have titled 'Honest
    John',
Who travelled afar in days bygone
The fight by Parnell made to shun,
Who hath stood recruiting plat-
    forms on,
And in lofty accents oft did prate,
Of a certain No Far Distant Date,
And always and ever did obey
The behests of the orator, Tay Pay,
Who went to beg money beyond
    the say,
And who holds an undisputed sway
Over the Party that fought and won,
And spoke and denounced the
    savage Hun,
To the great amusement of *Irish Fun*,
On the 'flure' of the House that
    Jack built.

This is the Mighty Atom, Joe,
Who tried with his Board of Erin O,
Dissension in our land to sow,
Who bids us all stand to attention,
And await the verdict of his
Convention,
Who doth conspire with the peer-
    less one,
Whom men have titled 'Honest
    John',
Who hath stood recruiting plat-
    forms on,
And in lofty accents oft did prate,
Of a certain No Far Distant Date,
And always and ever did obey
The behests of the orator, Tay Pay,
Who went to beg money beyond
    the say,
And who holds an undisputed sway
Over the Party that fought and won,
And spoke and denounced the
    savage Hun,
To the great amusement of *Irish Fun*,
On the 'flure' of the House that
    Jack built.

This is the coming General Election
That is giving the Party food for
    reflection.
That will for ever sweep away,
Knaves like the orator, Tay Pay,
And show the world that Ireland's
    sons,
Mean to get rid of her Honest Johns;
And the Mighty Atom they call Wee
    Joe
Will also have to pack and go.
They'll all lament at the doleful
    news
That they can no longer air their
    views
Where they fancied they had
    fought and won,
Where they warned and threatened
    the savage Hun,
To the great amusement of *Irish Fun*,
On the 'flure' of the House that
    Jack built.

Cited in Terry Moylan, *The indignant muse: poetry and songs of the Irish revolution, 1887–1926* (Dublin, 2016), 548–9.

●

Left: 'We kill all our own'—an anti-war, anti-John Redmond poster. (NLI)

1916–18 CHANGED UTTERLY

On 14 December 1918 the election that changed Ireland forever took place.

67

COVER: Éamon de Valera arriving back in Ireland in June 1917 after imprisonment in Pentonville Gaol. (UCD Archive)

BACK COVER: A memorable slogan on a poster from the South Longford by-election of May 1917. Joseph McGuinness became the first elected Sinn Féin MP. (NLI)

1916-18 CHANGED UTTERLY

EDITORIAL

EDITORS
John Gibney, Tommy Graham and
Georgina Laragy

EDITORIAL BOARD
...Canavan
...Collins
...Collins
...Fitzgerald
...Hanley
...Mitchell
... Ó Ciardha
... O'Flaherty
...as O'Loughlin

PUBLISHING MANAGER
...well

...
...land

...SETTING
...ondit

...ED IN IRELAND BY
... Baird Ltd.

...tory Ireland annual
...PUBLISHED BY HISTORY
...ICATIONS LTD 2017,
...9, 78 Furze Road, Sandyford
...ial Estate, Dublin 18.
...53 1) 2933568
... (+ 353 1) 2939377
W. www.historyireland.com

ISBN 978-0-9935328-1-8
First published 2017

The publisher gratefully acknowledges the
generous financial assistance of Glasnevin
Trust in the publication of this volume.

Preface

After last year's centenary commemorations of the 1916 Rising, with an impressive range and variety of events organised the length and breadth of the country, the ongoing 'Decade of Centenaries', in the eyes of the wider public at least, takes a back seat until the anniversaries of the December 1918 general election and the convening of the first Dáil Éireann in January 1919. Isn't the narrative of the intervening period well enough understood? The executions of the 1916 leaders provoked nationalist opinion, previously indifferent or even hostile to the separatist cause; public opinion was further provoked by a botched attempt to extend conscription to Ireland, which undermined support for Redmond's Irish Parliamentary Party and the prospect of Home Rule, about to be realised, and delivered a landslide victory to Sinn Féin in 1918. What is there to explain? Why have a special *History Ireland* supplement covering the June 1916 to December 1918 period?

Recent scholarship would suggest a more complex picture, but such scholarship more often than not appears in (often expensive) monographs or as articles in academic journals. How is the wider history-reading public to keep pace? That's where *History Ireland* comes in: 'to make the latest research accessible to the widest possible audience', according to our original mission statement of spring 1993. If the positive reception of our *1916: dream & death* supplement is anything to go by, this approach has proven popular with readers. We were fortunate to have had as contributors to that publication such well-known and established historians as Roy Foster, Joe Lee and Brian Murphy, as well as Emmet O'Connor, Pádraig Yeates, John Gibney and Mary McAuliffe, who also feature in this supplement. It will, we hope, not only give a flavour of the latest scholarship but also showcase the talents of a (slightly!) younger generation of historians such as Fearghal McGarry, Liz Gillis, Marie Coleman, Richard McElligott, Conor Mulveagh and Brian Hanley, to name but a few.

Of course, over this period the Great War rumbled on, with an undiminished scale of carnage that dwarfed anything produced by the 1916 Rising or the subsequent (consequent?) War of Independence or Civil War. That aspect— the ongoing influence of the Great War on Ireland—is not neglected here. Of particular significance was the entry into the war of the United States on the Allied side in April 1917 and the promulgation in January 1918 of President Woodrow Wilson's Fourteen Points, including the right of nations to self-determination. Such a mandate was delivered by the Irish electorate in December 1918 but sadly ignored. But *sin scéal eile* and raises issues that will be tackled in our next supplement, planned for early 2019.

***

I was joined on the editorial side by John Gibney and Georgina Laragy (both of Glasnevin Trust), without whose considerable scholarship, hard work and attention to detail this supplement would not have been produced. This would not have been possible without the cooperation of the board of Glasnevin Trust, and in particular of its CEO, George McCullough, who also provided a generous subvention. A word of thanks, too, for the provision of images by the staff of our efficient, but sadly underfunded, national institutions—the National Museum of Ireland (Finbarr Connolly in particular) and the National Library of Ireland (Berni Metcalfe in particular), as well as Aoife Torpey (Kilmainham Gaol) and Brian Kirby (Irish Capuchin Provincial Archives). Every effort has been made to obtain permission for the reproduction of images that may be subject to copyright; if we have erred in that regard, please get in touch and we will rectify the situation in later editions.

Tommy Graham

HISTORY IRELAND